Felicity Bryan

A Memoir

First published in Great Britain in 2022
by the Duncan and Bryan family,
in partnership with whitefox publishing

Copyright © the Duncan and Bryan family

www.wearewhitefox.com

ISBN 978-1-915635-03-7

Designed and typeset by Typo•glyphix
Cover design by Emma Ewbank
Project management by whitefox
Printed and bound by PrintCenter.com.tr, Istanbul

Contents

Foreword

Felicity Bryan was best known as one of Britain's leading literary agents, but she packed an extraordinary life with adventure and her many passions – literature, journalism, ballet and opera, art and gardening – and her deep friendships and loving family. Physically small but bursting with energy, she was once described by a friend as 'a June-bug on amphetamines'. She was imaginative and creative, generous-spirited and courageous, and was incapable of wasting time.

Nina Darnton, a writer she first befriended in the US, said, 'When I think of Felicity I think of lightning. A brilliant flash cutting through the sky electrified and electrifying everything near it ... She was kind, thoughtful, comforting when comfort was called for, clear-sighted and determined when that was necessary, meticulous in her planning for the future and in her remembering and honouring the past.'

'Few people had more friends,' one of her authors, David Pilling, wrote in her *Financial Times* obituary. 'She tended them over decades and loved them the way Charles Dickens loved the characters in his novels.' She was always attentive to what people needed or wanted and used her imagination and practicality to do something about it. She brought people together for great garden parties for which she often single-handedly prepared food for well over 100 guests.

Her dedication to authors and friends was matched by her energy and attention to her family. She said her mother had wanted her children to have 'the sunniest possible childhoods', and she in turn created this for her own children, Alice, Max and Ben. To them, she was supportive, dynamic and a lot of fun: she encouraged them, taught them to plant miniature gardens and sewed elaborate costumes for fancy dress parties at 5.00 a.m., while simultaneously hunting for a rental villa for the next mass family holiday.

She had to deal with much adversity. When Felicity was young, her mother, Betty, died after years of suffering from bipolar disorder, which put huge strain on the family. Felicity's daughter, Alice, developed the same illness in her teens and committed suicide at the age of 22. Both of her sisters died early from cancer, and she herself endured four cancers. All these gave a depth to her but did not extinguish her spark, and they reinforced her will to live life to the fullest.

———— ⬦ ————

Felicity was born in 1945, the daughter of Paul Bryan, a Conservative MP, and Betty Hoyle, a dynamic and loving mother. She grew up on a working farm on the edge of the Yorkshire Moors with her two sisters, Elizabeth and Bernadette. She did not enjoy school (where she was the naughtiest girl) but went on to study History of Art at the Courtauld Institute, a subject that remained a life-long passion.

At the age of 22 she headed to the US, where she embarked on a career in journalism with the *Financial Times* in Washington, making close friendships with leading journalists that lasted the rest of her life. Later, in 1979, in memory of Laurence Stern, her partner with whom she lived in Washington, she co-founded the Stern Fellowship, which annually for 40 years has sent a young British journalist to work at the *Washington Post*. Just before her death in 2020, she was deeply moved to hear that the *Washington Post* had renamed it the Stern-Bryan Fellowship in her honour.

In 1970 Felicity returned to London to work for the *Economist* on their American Survey, also initiating a series of Arts Briefs, and writing an extended survey on Wales, giving rise to a lifelong passion for Welsh rugby. Her love of nature expressed itself through her weekly gardening column for the *Evening Standard*, and through later writing two books, *The Town Gardener's Companion* and *A Garden for Children*.

In 1973 she was head-hunted by Curtis Brown, the literacy agency, where she worked for 15 years, becoming a director. In 1988 she founded her own agency – Felicity Bryan Associates (FBA) – in Oxford. Over the next three decades it grew to become the largest and most successful agency in Britain outside London, staffed entirely by women.

In her many years as an agent, Felicity represented everyone from historians, scientists and journalists, to cooks, ballet dancers and novelists. Among her many bestsellers and prize-winners were Karen

Armstrong's *A History of God*, Rosamunde Pilcher's *The Shell Seekers*, Roy Strong's *The Story of Britain*, Edmund de Waal's *The Hare with Amber Eyes*, Iain Pears' *An Instance of the Fingerpost*, Diarmaid MacCulloch's *A History of Christianity: The First Three Thousand Years* and Mary Berry's many popular cookery books.

Felicity loved spotting a gap in the market, or hearing ideas from editors and finding just the right author to write the book. Catherine Clarke, who took over as managing director of FBA, said Felicity had a 'visionary pragmatism ... The instincts that made her a good journalist – curiosity, dogged pursuit of a story, working the room like a small glittering star at parties – were perfect for her agenting life.' She was exhilarated by working with creative people, and she adored making connections, her natural talent for matchmaking being key to her success.

She also had a perceptiveness and clarity that helped her immediately see a book's value, and she would often provide insights on how the author could improve it. 'Beneath all that vigorous enthusiasm,' said her author Karen Armstrong, 'Felicity had what Matthew Arnold called "high seriousness". She quite simply changed my life ... the more I saw of Felicity, the more I understood that writing required the integrity and sincerity that was so evident in herself.'

She was fiercely protective of her clients. 'Felicity liked to say she was a lioness, not for herself, but for her authors,' Catherine Clarke said. David Pilling described how she 'fussed over her flock of authors like a mother duck'. Karen Armstrong recalled how 'Just two days before she died, she emailed me, triumphant and joyous at 2 o'clock in the morning during what she called her "morphine break", to tell me that the American deal for my new book had come through successfully. You would have thought that that would have been the last thing on her mind, but that extraordinary courage, transcendence of self and concern for others remained vibrant right to the end.'

———◇———

In the summer of 2019, Felicity was diagnosed with a type of stomach cancer that is notoriously hard to detect. Often, as in her case, when the cancer is found it has gone beyond the point at which it can be eradicated.

She therefore set about using her time well. She immediately prepared a To Do list. She began this memoir. She gave a big summer party in her garden. She worked with her colleagues at FBA to ensure that all her authors would be well looked after once she had died. She travelled twice to Spain to see her son Max. She went to the Jaipur Literary Festival with her friend and author Lindsey Hilsum, and revelled in the parties. In her final weeks, she started a series of weekly emails to promote books by her authors whose launch events had to be cancelled owing to the COVID-19 pandemic.

She kept the knowledge of her illness to a small group of people, but about two months before she died she judged the time was right to let the news spread more widely. She received hundreds of messages of farewell, she herself replying to those she could, and dictating replies to Ben and Max when she could no longer write.

She had an NHS bed in the conservatory, looking out over her garden. Two days before she died, elegantly dressed and with flowers in her hair, she received an MBE. She said she was happy, and died at home on 21 June 2020 – the summer solstice – without fear, and surrounded by her family.

———⟨⟩———

This memoir covers the period from when she left school in the early 1960s to her marriage to Alex in 1981. Years before, she had written an account of her childhood at Park Farm. Her time at school was undistinguished, so she thought she had little of interest to say. The period from 1981, covering her family life and her founding of the literary agency, she felt was well covered, not least by her photo albums.

Alex, Max and Ben Duncan
February 2022

1.

Introduction

In late June 2019 I learned that my life would be short: that the laparoscopy had shown my stomach cancer had spread. I had linitis plastica, a cruel cancer of the stomach lining, which does not show up on scans and announces itself when it has moved to neighbouring organs. Chemo would arrest the growth but would not stop it. I shall never forget the young surgeon's distressed expression as he said, 'I am so, so sorry. It's really bad.' I felt quite protective of him. 'How long have I got?' I said. He replied, 'It can come quite fast; on average it's a year.'

My husband, Alex, has seen me through three cancers (two breast and a melanoma) and I knew he would respond and be his stalwart self. 'I had imagined you as an old lady being like your grandmother Mardy,' he said wistfully. At this point I knew I had become his project until I die. Nothing will be too much.

We decided not to tell anyone but our very closest friends and my immediate family and colleagues at work. I wanted to continue to act as normal as possible while having my chemotherapy treatment. This was lucky because, as it turned out, I took well to the chemo in its three weekly cycles, began eating again and gained weight and energy. We had a magical summer visiting our son Max and his partner, Aritz, in Madrid, staying in France with Andrew and Harriet Nurnberg and in Tuscany for the wedding of our special friend Rachael Barraclough. Very few people were aware of my condition.

Early in July Andrew Nurnberg was visiting me at my office in Oxford. I asked him to arrive early so we could talk alone. He and I have worked closely together for 32 years, orchestrating the international rights in my authors' books. There is little about my business he does not know. Andrew's only sibling had died of ovarian cancer so he knows the form. He listened carefully while I outlined my situation. He was visibly grieved. Then he said the most wonderful thing: 'Bryan! If you dropped dead tomorrow people would say, "She had a FANTASTIC life!" Look what you have achieved,' he said, waving his arms around our capacious offices. Whereupon he sat down and sang my praises – my work, my children, my authors, my work team, etc. 'We are so privileged,' he said, 'us agents, working alongside such talented people. You have been amazing!' That is when I decided to write a memoir.

Philip Pullman, when interviewed on TV, said that everyone should be able to give an account of their life in a story. I had told the story of *My Childhood at Park Farm* in Yorkshire in a little book I made for the seven-year-old daughter of the family who had bought our family home. My schooldays were not a happy or memorable time. Most of our history as a family after Alex and I married in October 1981 is preserved in numerous photo albums. It's the period between leaving school in 1963 and getting married to Alex in 1981 that is only in my head and in letters I own. So that is the time on which I am concentrating. In the process I am finding out extraordinary things that happened to people I knew. It is a revelation and a re-living and I hope I reach the end.

2.

Leaving School 1962

I n summer 1962, at the age of 16, I left school and life proper – i.e. a life over which I had some control – began. I had not starred at school. My sister Libby had. My mother had had the annoying instinct of taking me out of a previous school in order that I could overlap with Libby. Thus it was that, aged eight, I was sent to Duncombe Park boarding school in Yorkshire where Libby was head girl and later was whisked out of that school early to overlap again with Libby, who at that point was deputy head girl of Benenden School in Kent.

Libby liked this arrangement even less than I. For wherever I went, I was not only the smallest girl in the school but also the naughtiest – and a source of embarrassment and irritation to Libby as I egged on my small friends to ignore her orders.

The only thing I retained from my Duncombe Park days of twice daily chapel was an almost complete knowledge of *Hymns A&M* – which has stuck – and of wild flowers – which has stuck less well. From Benenden I retain my friendship with Thalia Myers, a talented pianist, who – like me – could not wait to leave. We would sneak off to the music block with the *Noël Coward Song Book* from which she played lyrically and we sang 'Chase Me Charlie', 'I'll See You Again' and 'A Room with a View' and felt for that short time lifted from the regimen of dreary rule-based school. The rest of my happy hours were spent in the Art Studio, encouraged by a sweet Miss Cox.

Because we were dying to leave, both Thalia and I and a handful of others opted to only stay for a year in the sixth form. To our delight we were allowed to take A-levels in one year. We were well taught in this smaller class and thus it was that, to my surprise and to the almost insulting amazement of my family, I in August received a note to say that I had achieved good grades in my A-levels in History, English Literature and History of Art. And thus I had my first useful qualification.

It's worth pausing now to describe the family to whom I returned that summer. We looked like a very normal, happy family with mother Betty, father Paul, my widowed grandmother Mardy, 20-year-old Elizabeth (Libby), who had wanted to be a doctor from the age of six and was now training at St Thomas' in London, and Bernadette (Bunny), aged 13, who was now at school with me. We lived at Park Farm on the edge of the Yorkshire Moors and us girls spent a lot of our time haring around Wykeham Forest on our shaggy ponies, Gypsy and Beauty.

But all was not as it seemed. Two years before, my brilliant, lively, creative, warm-hearted mother had been diagnosed with manic depression. She had already attempted suicide once and had suffered acute depressions when she had to be hospitalised. They were horrifying. My mother became a helpless stranger to me, lying with her face to the wall and unable to communicate.

But the manic stage was even more scary. As she emerged from depression – often with the help of electric shock treatment – we would have a period of normality where she gained the old spirit we had lost. Then suddenly she would start behaving in a riotous way that was difficult to control. She would write long, insulting letters to people – I once received 25 sides from her telling me what a tart I was – would go on spending sprees, would wake up in the middle of the night and start painting the kitchen baby blue with pans to match. She lost all sense of reason and was impossible to communicate with. She could not be left safely alone.

My father adored my mother. He was as mystified by her illness as we children. He was MP for the constituency of Howden and, at that time, was vice-chairman of the Conservative Party in charge of candidates – a job he was extremely good at. He had entered Parliament as the MP for Howden in 1955 along with Tony Barber and Willie Whitelaw and had been the first of his lot to become a Parliamentary Private Secretary and then a whip. His star was on the rise when my mother's illness struck. Now his priority had to be to look after her.

Libby was living with my father in our flat in Marsham Court, Westminster, and was thus able to help quite a bit. And later she heroically took a year out from medical school to look after Mummy. All this needs telling because it explains how very free I was to do what I liked – including leaving school early. Unlike many teenagers, I had no authority figure to rebel against. My father was only relieved when

I made my own arrangements. The previous January I had answered an ad in *The Times* to go on an Erna Low skiing holiday in Villars-sur-Ollon. I knew nobody on the trip but had a high old time meeting this odd assortment of people, sharing a bedroom with the glamorous and much more sophisticated Rampling sisters – Sarah and Charlotte – who very much took me under their wing and taught me how to dance the twist.

When I left school I still had no clue what I wanted to do with my life. In fact, I was very envious of Libby, who had always known she wanted to be a doctor. I too would work hard if I knew what target I was aiming at. I remember saying to my mother that I wanted to find a career that was 'a way of life'.

My father's advice on my upbringing and future now depended quite a bit on the guidance of other Tory wives like my mother's great friend Celia Whitelaw. They – unlike my mother – tended not to have an interest in their daughters having careers but were more preoccupied in them 'coming out', doing the Season and then finding good husbands.

So that was why in September 1962 I had been booked for six months in Paris at a finishing school called Mademoiselle Anita, which was attached to a convent called La Villa de L'Assomption. Papa took me there and – while I settled in – spent days sitting in the Champs-Élysées, watching the world go by and having a well-deserved break from the anxious place that was our home.

Mlle Anita Pojninska's school was one to which young women went on leaving school to be polished up before facing the Season – or whatever. Most girls stayed with French families but I had fortunately been booked into a *pension famille*, a cheaper option where a family took in lots of lodgers who were much freer to come and go as they pleased. Mine was in the 16th arrondissement near La Muette metro, so a healthy walk to school or a convenient metro trip. I shared a room with a lively English girl called Rosemary – not a brilliant start for my French. But the other lodgers were Dutch, Spanish, etc., and so French was the common language in which we muddled by over our communal meals. I really liked it.

And I simply loved the very fact of being in Paris. Every morning we had lessons: French and French Literature, Philosophy, History of Art, etc. There were also mysterious sessions given by Mlle Anita herself called '*Savoir Vivre*' – the only bit of which I remember was her telling us '*Votre corps, c'est un temple*' – and another called '*Savoir Faire*', which was more about manners. Then in the afternoon there were expeditions around Paris and long sessions in the Louvre. Our teachers were very high grade and I adored my museum visits in the hands of experts who really taught you how to look at a painting. So my cup was full. I also made some good friends, including Caroline Ross, an enchanting girl with long dark hair and striking wide-apart eyes who was exactly my size – we have exchanged clothes ever since.

Like me, Caroline had left school at 16 with excellent A-levels. She spoke beautiful French already. But unlike me she did not have ambitions for a career. She was – and still is – extremely beautiful, with an engaging little-girl-lost look that made all men want to look after her – and more. She was staying with a Madame who introduced her on day one to a well-bred young Frenchman who, not surprisingly, wanted to escort Caroline everywhere.

So Caroline's social life was quite grand and definitely a cut above mine. My social life was mostly provided by Danny. Danielle had been our au pair helping at Park Farm one summer. She was now at the

Sorbonne. Her friends were lively students who spent their evenings on the Left Bank drinking and smoking Gauloises or Gitanes cigarettes. I remember a particular *boîte* in Rue Mouffetard where we would dance to Françoise Hardy singing '*Tous les garçons et les filles de mon age*' and crooning from Johnny Hallyday. Danny's friends were very international and a total change for me.

Back at my pension, I always had a friendly reception around the welcoming kitchen table. I can vividly remember us all sitting around that table watching the tiny TV in terror awaiting events during the Cuban Missile Crisis, when for a week in late October 1962 the US and the Soviet Union came close to nuclear war. As President Kennedy and Premier Khrushchev exchanged threats and Soviet missiles sailed towards Cuba to be faced by a US blockade, it genuinely did feel that the world as we knew it might come to an end.

I can't remember when the Eureka moment happened. But it was in Paris that I decided I wanted to go to university. I wanted to study History of Art. At that time there were few British universities where you could take such a degree. But research at the British Council showed me that Cambridge had a Part 2 degree so I could do Part 1: History and Part 2: History of Art. All I needed to do was get in. But to get in I needed to have an O-level in Latin, which I had not learned.

I came home for a weekend from Paris to see Libby as bridesmaid at the wedding of her friend Elizabeth Guthrie. I put the idea to Papa. He responded so positively, and phoned the excellent Gabbitas & Thring educational agency who found me a place at a crammer called Kirby Lodge in Little Shelford, just outside Cambridge. There I could do a crash six-month Latin course starting in January, continue with my

History and apply for Cambridge in the autumn. So my sojourn in Paris, which was meant to be six months, ended up as three. But it had at least made me decide that I did not want to be a debutante, that I wanted to go to university to read art history and therefore had a goal, and in Caroline Ross – later Caroline Weeks – I had made a friend for life.

Thus it was that in January I arrived in Little Shelford and there began my love affair with Cambridge. By great luck I actually enjoyed learning Latin, and *Georgics IV* – all about gardens and bees – was just up my alley. My teacher was encouraging. I lived in digs with a wonderful, warm family. The father was a gardener who had been captured by the Japanese and worked on the Burma Railway in the war – as had many of the Cambridgeshire Regiment – and had never been able to work indoors again. They had two young children and made me feel very at home.

In digs next door was Tricia Cockcroft, already engaged in studying History for A-level. She came from Todmorden in the West Riding of Yorkshire, not far from Hebden Bridge of my early childhood. So that was a link. And we immediately became friends. She made me laugh a lot, and still does. She was also a voracious reader of fiction – and still is. She introduced me to her brother Laurie, a tall, blond young man with a breezy manner and a great laugh. He was a very inspiring person to me. He had done Voluntary Service Overseas (VSO) in Africa and seemed much more worldly than some of the other undergraduates I was meeting. He was studying at St John's and was sharing digs with Tim Lankester, also a VSO veteran. Their flat in St John's Street was a social whirl. I met so many lively undergraduates there. Tim played the piano and I remember sing-alongs with Celia Hadden and Nicky Brooke – who later surprised us all by getting pregnant at Cambridge and having a baby out of wedlock.

I would often have coffee with Laurie at the Whim – a café near the Seeley Library – the university history library where I regularly went to study and also to meet other undergraduates. So my social life was fun. At a party in 'the drains' – a basement area in King's College – I met a group mostly from King's. I remember Simon Perry and his friend Carey Harrison (son of famous Rex and Lilli Palmer) and spending a sunny morning with them reading the *Sunday Times* in King's College garden and the scandals of Christine Keeler and the government minister John Profumo, which had rocked the nation. Simon was to later introduce me to ballet and opera, for which I had so much to thank him. Also in that party in the drains I met Nick Jardine, who was later to become my boyfriend.

One day I was invited to a punting party by Anthony Hulbert, the elder brother of Victoria, one of my friends from Paris. On it was a very jolly Scottish lawyer called Derry Irvine with a girlfriend and his great friend Charles Morland. Charlie was particularly warm and fun. These men were an older group than my normal undergraduate friends as they had all spent two years doing National Service in the army after school and thus seemed more mature.

The summer continued on, I took my Latin O-level and two other O-levels, giving me a splendid 11. I also re-took History A-level, adding a scholarship-level paper, which Tricia also took. One of the questions was about our local town and its history. She did Todmorden and I did Hebden Bridge. The mill towns we were describing were very parallel.

So we emerged with our grades. By the time the results came in I was having a heavenly summer in London, largely with Charlie Morland. I was still hooked on studying History of Art but London was alluring and I decided that rather than go back to Cambridge and do university entrance I would apply for the Courtauld Institute of Art – the top place to take an undergraduate degree in the subject and a part of London University.

So you could say that I followed a man to London. My poor father had the embarrassment of revealing that I would not be returning to Kirby Lodge. I applied to the Courtauld and started mugging up on Gombrich's brilliant *The Story of Art* and many other art books in the Westminster Library. I also earned money as a cleaning lady through a company called Universal Aunts and got a job working for an ecclesiastical furnishing company whose name I don't recall. I did a part-time shorthand and typing course at Pitman. In those days many girls were encouraged to do this 'just in case' they needed to earn money as a secretary – boys never did.

Charlie and I did not continue as an 'item'. He had started working at the Foreign Office – his father was an ambassador and his brother Martin was already flying high there. I went to a party at Martin's flat and there was Charlie positively curled around a very pretty girl called Victoria and I knew my time was up. So my real reason for abandoning Cambridge entrance was gone. But I did not mind as I was enjoying London so much.

In and among all this I was having some fun on the fringes of the London Season. My parents were giving a 'coming out' dance for me in Yorkshire in August and I had been invited to many tea parties in the spring by the mothers of other girls who were coming out. As I remember, you arrived at some smart flat – probably in Kensington or Knightsbridge – and sat on the floor having tea and chatting to other girls and exchanging addresses with the ones you liked and you wanted to come to your dance or cocktail party. I went to many dances in London largely dressed in long garments that I had made with the help of our family friend Margaret Beale, affectionately known as Muggs, who had taught me to sew. Muggs made my rather wonderful deep blue Thai silk coming-out dress.

The biggest draw for me in London was Covent Garden. I had always loved ballet from when I was a child. But now in London I became hooked. Simon Perry and his friend Nicholas Payne and others used to come down from Cambridge at regular intervals to queue overnight on the pavement at Covent Garden and get tickets for the next 'booking period'. I became part of this gang, arriving with my sleeping bag. We would also book for opera, which was becoming a growing passion of mine. My favourite seat was CC1 – the one ticket in the 'slips' in the 'gods' upstairs that faced forward – for about six shillings.

Everyone of my generation can remember where they were on 22 November 1963, the night that President John F. Kennedy was killed. I was in a passenger seat being driven up to Yorkshire by a local friend called Fred Procope. We were listening to the radio and the programme was interrupted by the news that the President had been shot in Dallas, Texas. It was not known if he had survived. Then on the Doncaster bypass Fred's Mini hit the kerb. The next thing I knew I was coming to by the roadside in our bashed-up car and asking what had happened to John Kennedy. By the time I was in York Hospital with a broken collar-bone we knew that he was dead.

I remember lying in bed at Park Farm in shock. Kennedy was such a hero to me. I also remember feeling frustrated that I could not return to London immediately, for the following week I was meant to be going to Covent Garden to see the new Russian star Rudolf Nureyev dance with Margot Fonteyn in 'The Shades' from *La Bayadère*, which he had introduced into the repertoire for her. I was also going to miss the performance of a new group, the Beatles, who were still making a name for themselves, on 26 November at the Regal Cinema in Cambridge ...

Looking back, it's extraordinary what amazing ballet and opera I saw at Covent Garden in those years between 1962 and 1968. It was a real heyday for the Royal Ballet. Of course there was the excitement of Nureyev's arrival, which brought Margot Fonteyn out of near retirement. I saw their first *Swan Lake* and *Giselle* together and their premiere of Kenneth MacMillan's *Romeo and Juliet* in 1965 where they had 43 curtain calls. The sad thing was that the ballet had been conceived and created by MacMillan for the brilliant and quirky young ballerina Lynn Seymour and her regular partner, the boyish Christopher Gable. But the powers that be insisted that Fonteyn and Nureyev were a bigger draw and must have the first night. I remember watching Seymour in the role – in particular the extraordinary episode where she sits motionless on the bed as Prokofiev's music churns, reflecting the torment in her head before going to Friar Laurence – and crying my eyes out. I think by now I must have seen that production at least 15 times.

In opera I saw the stupendous Joan Sutherland many times including twice in *Lucia di Lammermoor*. I was dotty about Tito Gobbi and saw him as Scarpia in *Tosca* on many occasions, usually paired with Marie Collier, and as the most brilliant Iago in a production of *Otello* – with

Joan Carlyle and James McCracken – which I must have seen five times. Pavarotti was just beginning to make appearances, as was his friend Maria Freni. I remember a glorious *Traviata* created by Visconti in 1967, where Freni sang Violetta with heart-breaking warmth. After the first night Nicky Payne phoned me. Would I contribute to a fund to have the production recorded from Radio 3 later in the week? I did and still have the rather scratched vinyl record.

My big regret was that I never saw Maria Callas. She was still appearing – but rarely – at Covent Garden and in 1964 had sung *Tosca* directed by Franco Zeffirelli with Tito Gobbi. I had somehow missed that. But they were bringing it back in 1965, and I queued three nights and two days to buy my rationed two tickets (friends would sit in my patch while I went off to lectures). Triumphantly I offered one of my two tickets to Muggs. She had been a constant in our lives during our childhood, as my mother's best friend and Libby's godmother. She was very glamorous but had never married – which somehow made her even more exotic to us. She adored music and played the piano very well. During the war, when she was a nurse in Australia, she had had an affair with the striking conductor Malcolm Sargent. She had taught Bunny and me the 'Dance of the Cygnets' from *Swan Lake*. She lived at Stonegate in Sussex in a quaint oast house with round brick towers and used to come and take us out from school. She taught me to sew, which was how she made her living. And while she sewed she listened to opera.

So Muggs was a perfect recipient for my precious extra ticket. She was so excited and we plotted our evening. But it was not to be. A few days before the performance, Callas backed out, pleading sickness. Many people felt that she was nervous, now she was over 40, that she was no longer up to the role. The disappointment was huge. She was my heroine and I realised I would never hear her in the flesh. Why had I not saved up the money and gone with Nicky Payne on an expedition to hear her in Paris (Nicky was always arranging jaunts like that)? I had thought it too pricey at the time. As it was, Muggs and I saw the lovely Marie Collier in the Callas role and Gobbi was his brilliant self.

3.

The Courtauld Institute

C ome the spring of 1964, I sat for my Courtauld interview in the imposing and beautiful Home House designed by Robert Adam at 20 Portman Square. The director of the Courtauld was – the later notorious – Professor Sir Anthony Blunt, who was also the Keeper of the Queen's Pictures. The interview took place in his splendid office on the top floor. There he sat at the centre of a long table flanked by John Shearman, George Zarnecki, Michael Kitson, Peter Murray, Peter Kidson and other luminaries of the art historical establishment with whom I was familiar from their books, making a 'Last Supper' formation. And over the fireplace there was a Poussin ...

Faced with this distinguished assortment, I was unsurprisingly nervous. We talked about what I planned to read and then they started handing me photographs of works of art to identify. I was doing quite well until I made them giggle by describing a sarcophagus as a 'sarka-faargi' – all my learning was from books – and had a hot flush when corrected. Then I was presented with a photo of what I was convinced was a painting by Giorgione. 'It's a Correggio,' said John Shearman dismissively. 'It's in the National Gallery.' Hot flush again. By the time I was through, I was convinced I had failed and proceeded to pass clean out in the ornate marble bathroom, which was the lair of Anthony Blunt's secretary. She bought me to with sal volatile – and I am sure was responsible for passing a kind word to the director.

Some weeks later, while I was still awaiting my results, my grandmother suggested that she give Pa and me a treat and sent us out for an evening at Old Vienna, a favourite London haunt of hers, where you ate Wiener schnitzel and were yodelled to by waiters in lederhosen. Off we duly went and when we sat down Pa asked for champagne. It was opened and he slyly congratulated me on getting into the Courtauld. I looked stunned. He had phoned them in the morning, said he was taking me out to dinner and it would be so lovely to know if he had to cheer me up or congratulate me. Blunt's secretary gave him the news that I had got in. So that was that. It was so typical of my lovely father to do that. I immediately abandoned the Pitman's secretarial course and booked myself into a course to learn Italian at the British Institute in Florence.

That summer in Florence was glorious. I had been studying the work of Italian artists for quite a time by now but had never been to Italy. I remember my very first weekend, taking myself off alone to Ravenna because I just could not wait to see the sixth-century Byzantine mosaics of Justinian and Theodora at San Vitale in Classe, which had so bewitched me in books.

The British Institute was housed in the Palazzo Antinori, built in the mid-fifteenth century by the family of famous Florentine wine producers. It was at the north end of the fashionable Via de' Tornabuoni. The ground floor housed the Antinori wine offices and upstairs we took our classes. My fellow students were an interesting selection, including Peter Turrini, an Irish-Italian who sang in the chorus at Covent Garden and with whom I hit it off right away, talking opera gossip. Our classes were all in the morning and then we were free to explore.

Initially I stayed with a family in the suburbs but this was no fun and quite expensive. Soon I paired up with some fellow students, including a young South African law student called Alan Dashwood, and took a flat in Borgo San Frediano on the south side of the Arno River that runs through Florence. It was up five flights but had a great view when you got to the terrace at the top. I loved housekeeping there and beginning to make simple Italian meals with spaghetti and other pastas, and delicious salads, so unlike the food I was accustomed to in England.

Many weekends I went away with fellow students and stayed in youth hostels. We climbed to the heights of Assisi, visited the frescoes by Giotto in Padua and went to the Palio in Siena where – after a brilliant medieval procession – ten horses raced around the exquisite central Piazza del Campo. I particularly loved Siena.

Another weekend I went to the Spoleto Festival. I had not previously heard of it but its attraction to me was that Fonteyn and Nureyev were to dance there, performing the full three acts of *La Bayadère*. I managed to get a couple of tickets and Alan and I planned to stay at the youth hostel in Spoleto. A week or so before the performance, Fonteyn's husband, Roberto Arias, was shot in Panama. She rushed from London to Panama and cancelled her visit to Spoleto. She was replaced by Annette Page, a regular dancer at the Royal Ballet, who I had seen perform. I was of course disappointed but I was also sorry for Annette Page. When we had settled in Spoleto, I went to look for a florist shop so I could send her flowers on the night. Florists were sparse and all I could find were a bunch of greenish carnations, which I handed in at the stage door on arrival.

The performance proceeded. Nureyev positively flew through the air in this ballet of which I had only seen the last act before. And Annette Page danced enchantingly. After the performance I went round to the stage door and asked if I could see Miss Page to whom I had sent the flowers. We were let in and I knocked on her door. There stood my strange green flowers. We had a little conversation about my having watched her at Covent Garden and then I went out. Then I noticed the next door was open. There stood Nureyev. He was chatting and laughing with some Italian men who had given him a scarf, which he was playing with. I introduced myself as a fan from London and asked him to sign my programme, which he did with a flourish. As I walked out I noticed someone else in the room. It was Noël Coward in the corner, smiling on the scene. Later we had coffee together in the piazza, which was a treat for me – and something I couldn't wait to report to my father, whose favourite song was 'I'll See You Again'.

———✧———

Come October 1964 my studies began. Sometimes I think that if I had to re-run my life I would not have studied in London. While I had a high old time during my three years at the Courtauld, I did have all my life to be in London and I never really experienced a campus life. My fellow students were an interesting bunch, but we all lived miles apart from each other so did not experience the camaraderie that I would have had at Cambridge or Sussex – somewhere I had contemplated.

As art history was not commonly taught at undergraduate level, at least half of the undergraduates had started life studying something else, be it History or Engineering, and then seen the light and opted to do either an undergraduate or master's degree at the Courtauld. Nearly all of them saw themselves as having a career in the world of art history, whether in museums, teaching or academia. They were an extremely dedicated lot. During the first year we did a very broad course from Minoans to Picasso, attending lectures every day, and alongside we had tutorial groups of four to five in which we did our 'special subjects': Rembrandt with Michael Kitson in the first term, London's eighteenth-century architecture with John Murray, etc., on which we wrote our essays. And how privileged we were. Analysing a Rembrandt etching with Michael Kitson or studying a Mantegna drawing with John Shearman was an experience that sent tingles down my spine. There was no doubt that I had chosen a subject that could become my way of life.

At the end of the year we took our prelims exams before specialising further in the next two years. I had opted to study the fifteenth century, which was mostly Italian and Flemish art. That first year I was living in my parents' flat at Marsham Court in Westminster. My father was still working at Conservative Party Central Office as vice chairman of the party in charge of candidates. My mother was not well, spending her time either at a psychiatric hospital in Virginia Water or at home with my grandmother in Yorkshire or in London. The London periods could be frightening and it was when I was revising for my prelims that things got really bad. She was in a manic state, worrying all the time and saying she dare not be left alone in case she threw herself over the balcony. As she had already attempted suicide this was no empty threat. It was a very stressful time for me and for my father.

I remember in June 1965 going to see John Shearman – the great Raphael expert – who was to be my tutor for fifteenth-century Italian art the following year. We were to talk about the programme. I heard myself saying, 'But there may not be a next year.' This shy man looked surprised. Then I found myself telling him about my mother and her frantic moods, how it was impossible to revise for my prelims at home and I was convinced I would fail my exams. He suddenly became extremely sympathetic. I later learned that he had known mental illness in his wife's family. He realised that the situation was impossible. He said that he could assure me that if I did fail my prelims I would be allowed to retake the first year. He would discuss it with his colleagues. His reassurance was enough. I managed to get through my prelims with a 2:1 and then headed off to Austria to learn some German.

Summer 1965

My Courtauld vacations were extremely lively. That first summer of 1965 I had booked myself into a German course in Salzburg for August but was planning to see Vienna first. Lucilla Kingsbury was a tall, elegant and fascinating girl in my year. She had spent the year before the Courtauld studying restoration at the Uffizi so had excellent Italian and seemed very sophisticated. She had no summer plans and was taken with the idea of Vienna. So off we headed by train together to stay in a B&B with Fraulein Helget in Lerchenfelderstrasse. Vienna was a spellbinding treat. The Kunsthistorisches Museum and other galleries quite bowled us over and we spent most of our days there. Lucilla had some rather smart connections and we were taken out to a very drunken evening in Grinzing, where the new wine knocked us out. Through these connections – which included the British ambassador – Lucilla found a summer job as an au pair in Vienna while I headed to Salzburg.

My course proved good and full of lively people – in particular some Italians. But my German never really took off as they all spoke English or French. I would meet up with Lucilla sometimes on weekends – I remember one at Melk and St Florian, glorious rococo monasteries on the Danube, another in Munich where we learned to love light beer, and again we immersed ourselves in the galleries.

Returning from Munich, we took the Vienna train, which stopped in Salzburg on the way. We were enjoying a light beer in the dining car when we got talking to an attractive-looking German in his early thirties called Fritz Rumler. He was a writer from *Der Spiegel* and was about to review some events at the Salzburg Festival. Lucilla looked a touch wistful as the train headed to Vienna where Fritz and I got off together. And with good reason. He proceeded to take me out to dinner and turned out to be an extraordinarily cultivated and interesting man. He asked if I was going to any events at the festival. I replied that of course I could not afford the major operas but I was going to small musical events. So that was how I got to see Karajan conducting Nicolai Ghiaurov in *Boris Godunov* – a famous production that was recorded.

Fritz also took me to a giddy-making lunch by the river with friends of his from the Bayerischer Rundfunk radio station. His world was just what I wanted to be part of. He was also the first German with whom I had talked deeply about what life was like for the post-war generation – he was born in 1932 – growing up among the secrets and the guilt. Years later I mentioned him to a German publisher friend who said Fritz was a very famous *Der Spiegel* writer who had covered every subject under the sun, but particularly theatre. I googled him. He remained all his life at *Der Spiegel* and had died in 2002. I read an extraordinary obituary, which showed a charming picture of him looking out at me across time and holding a book he had written on Shakespeare.

After a month in Salzburg the plan was to meet up with Caroline Ross in Vienna to head to Greece for September. Lucilla then decided that she would like to join us. This turned out to be lucky as Caroline arrived in Vienna with an army officer called Rufus in tow – so I would have felt quite left out. It was also lucky because Lucilla had already proved herself a wonderfully enthusiastic travelling companion. We had such fun together. We had so many shared enthusiasms. After some days in Athens we sailed with Caroline and Rufus to the island of Mykonos – then quite undeveloped with its striking windmills. There, Jock Campbell – an old Argentinian admirer of Caroline – showed us the island and introduced us to some fellow travellers who were heading off to Crete. So we parted with Caroline and Rufus and sailed to Delos, Syros, Santorini and finally Heraklion in Crete.

At the end of my month in Greece – which included visiting Corinth and hitch-hiking in the Peloponnese – I worked out that I had spent £11.00. While that meant more in those days, it was still pretty thrifty.

We slept on beaches near Knossos and in caves at Matala in the south of Crete near the ruins of Phaistos. At one point we worked in a grape packing factory in Heraklion and were invited to stay by a Cretan family working there. They introduced us to a friend who was the captain of the overnight ferry returning to Piraeus. So we hitched for free on that. I even sold a pint of my blood in Athens in order to buy presents to bring home ...

1966

In early 1966 I went on a pilgrimage to the Netherlands in search of my hero Rogier van der Weyden and other Flemish painters who, in my eyes, had quite outstripped the Italians in their amazing spirituality. Why I went via Paris I do not remember – probably another exhibition. But I do remember hitch-hiking from Paris to Brussels – where I was to meet up with my then boyfriend John, who was there on business. I can't even remember who I hitch-hiked with, but it must have been someone I met in a youth hostel. I do remember the extraordinary coldness of that road to Brussels with its biting wind as we waited for a lift and seeing signs to Mons and other battlefields of the First World War. I could not imagine the hell of being in a trench in that cold.

Brussels, once I got there, was much more exciting than I was prepared for and with John I ate thrilling meals and discovered frites with mayo. I then headed off on my own to Bruges and Ghent. I arrived in Bruges of an evening and the cold that I had picked up on that chilly northern French road was in full swing. At the information desk at Bruges Station they said there were no vacancies in hostels. I looked desperate and a kind man picked up the phone. Perhaps I would like to stay with *les belles soeurs?* So I ended up in a charming nunnery where the nuns took one look at me and tucked me up in a little cell with the most beautiful view of swans strutting along the icy canal outside.

Bruges enchanted me, and the paintings in Groeningemuseum – by Jan van Eyck, Hans Memling, Hugo van der Goes, Gerard David, Hieronymus Bosch – were everything I had hoped for. I then headed off to Ghent. I have been there twice since and still believe that van Eyck's *Adoration of the Lamb* altarpiece is one of the masterpieces of the world. From there I visited Antwerp in search of van der Weyden's *Seven Sacraments Altarpiece*, which has much of the feel of *The Descent from the Cross* in the Prado. But this was the first one I saw and I shall never forget it. It was the highlight of that trip.

When I got back to the London flat from Belgium there was a letter from my father. I phoned Park Farm. My mother had tried to take her life and had nearly succeeded by slashing both her wrists and her throat in the bathroom. I think it was Libby who found her. She had been rushed to Leeds hospital where they had some advanced machine that saved her life. She was now recovering. My father sounded so tired. He seemed almost at the end of his tether. I had never heard him sound like that before. And I found myself wishing that Mummy had died. I could not bear watching the effect that her mad illness had on my father and grandmother and on us all. What's more, there was no cure. We could be living with this forever.

Looking back on that period, the times that my mother was well or ill rather merge. There was quite a long period when she was at a mental hospital in Virginia Water called the Holloway – I think now part of Royal Holloway College. I would visit her by train from London. Sometimes she was quite calm and we could walk in the gardens together. Sometimes she was in bed. And sometimes she was having electric shock treatment, which calmed her but made her memory very poor. My father would visit her regularly and then there were periods when she would come home to Park Farm and seem pretty normal. She would garden away and see her friends. Then the depression or the manic phase would return. Mummy's closest girl friends like Muggs, my godmother Dorothy Davidson and Bridget Cramp, her great friend from her wartime days, were constant in their attention.

By now I had many friends in London. But a particular addition was my cousin David Wevill and his wife, Assia. David was a Canadian, the son of my father's sister Sylvia. He was ten years my senior and I remember him coming to stay at Park Farm before going to Cambridge. He looked like James Dean and was completely charming and I remember my eight-year-old self asking my mother if it was legal to marry your cousin.

After leaving Cambridge, David had worked in publishing but his real aim was to live as a poet. I was very proud of the fact that he was published in an edition of Penguin Modern Poets. My father's sister Margo, who was very conspiratorial and worked for MI6, used to tell us what

David was up to. There had been many girlfriends. But then in 1956 on a transatlantic liner he had met Assia and was smitten.

Assia was eight years older than him, and of German-Jewish descent. Her family had escaped Germany before the war and lived in Tel Aviv. She had married an Englishman and moved to London after the war, then to Canada, where she met her second husband. Then she met 21-year-old David and left her second husband and married David in 1960. They had lived in Mandalay in Burma for a while where David taught English. She spoke many languages and had a successful job as an advertising copywriter with J. Walter Thompson – a job she was very dismissive of but which paid the rent. They lived with their baby, Shura (born in March 1965), in an elegant flat in Swiss Cottage. I thought them the perfect couple. Their world of poets and writers was very much the world of which I wished to be a part – they were my Latin Quarter.

Assia was extremely warm and welcoming to me, as was David, and I would often visit them and have supper and play with baby Shura. We also had surprising friends in common in Martin Morland, who had lived in Burma as a diplomat, and Guy Slater, an actor friend of mine whose parents had been diplomats there too. One evening I dropped by on short notice. They were clearly preoccupied. There was a lot of luggage in the hall. They said they were moving but were vague about it. So I went off. Some six months later Assia phoned me out of the blue. She was in London with Shura. Could she come and stay? I said I was sorry but my mother was very ill so it was not possible but I would love to see her. The next day I visited her in Hampstead in the house of a couple called Mendelssohn. All was explained. The night I had visited was the night before she left David for her lover, the poet Ted Hughes, with whom she was now living in Devon.

Of course I knew of Ted Hughes, whose wife, the poet Sylvia Plath, had killed herself. What I did not know was that Assia had been his mistress and was by many people blamed for what happened to Plath. Assia talked about Ted. How strong he was and how boyish David seemed in comparison. She was clearly fraught and somewhat defensive. That was the last time I saw her. In 1969 I learned from Guy Slater that Assia had killed both herself and her child.

Russia

The summer of 1966 I visited Russia for the first time. I had always longed to go to the Hermitage to see the Rembrandts but did not think I stood a chance of getting there. Then I noticed an ad on the Courtauld notice board to join a student group going to Leningrad and Moscow in July. It was for just under two weeks and cost £40 – it was subsidised by Sputnik, which was the student version of Intourist, the state tourist service. Years later I realised that this was the period of thaw in the regime under Khrushchev, which began to allow contact with the West.

I arrived with an assortment of about 20 other students at Waterloo Station. We headed off by train to Warsaw where we were met by enthusiastic Polish students and put up in student accommodation. We coincided with Army Day, which meant I saw a mini Red Square parade complete with tanks, massed Warsaw Pact troops and the lot all marching in front of the 'Stalin Gothic' Palace of Culture and Science. Warsaw had been rebuilt from its wartime ashes very beautifully, I thought.

Then we headed on a very luxurious overnight train to Leningrad. This was a complete revelation. The Italianate architecture of the Hermitage and the Winter Palace with its strong southern colours against a very northern light quite blew me away. I remember sitting beside the Neva River at midnight and the sky was still light. To my surprise we were not over-supervised by our student hosts. There were many events in our itinerary but when I dropped out of the factory visit in favour of going again to the Hermitage there were no objections. On our first group visit to the Hermitage we were shown the Scythian gold treasure, which was a total revelation to me. My later visits on my own found me in heaven.

In my naivety and steeped in *Anna Karenina*, I had somehow thought that I might communicate in French. But in fact it was German that got me by – it was, after all, only just over 20 years since they were overrun. As long as I introduced myself as English and then spoke German, I got a very friendly response.

One night I went to see the Kirov Ballet dance *Swan Lake* in its amazing theatre. I sat upstairs beside a very sweet girl who spoke English. We saw that the czar's box bang in the centre of the grand tier was empty and so in the interval crept down and sat in it. The opera was also open and thus it was that I got myself a cheap ticket and attended my first Wagner opera, hearing *Lohengrin* in Russian. It was thrilling. It was also so enlightening at the height of the Cold War to find that my Russian neighbours at the opera or in the street were so warm and welcoming.

After days in Leningrad and its surroundings we headed overnight to Moscow and the same greeting from students. In Moscow I was lucky to have some contacts as Granada TV, where my godfather Denis Forman worked, had made a series on the fiftieth anniversary of the October Revolution. He gave me the name of a Russian TV friend with a very sweet wife who invited me out to their dacha on a weekend. It was in a compound for writers and theatre people and I realised that if you did toe the line you could have some good aspects to life. I was interested that all of their friends had read Pasternak and other forbidden writers. I remember it as a magic day. We swam in the river nearby and my hostess admired my matching bra and pants in black and white check. When I got back to England I sent her some. But I never knew if they arrived.

While I was in Moscow, having an amazing time in the museums, England won the football World Cup against West Germany. The Russians were jubilant and kept chanting, 'Bobby Charlton! Bobby Charlton!' The museum that particularly amazed me was the Tretyakov Gallery of Russian art. I was completely unaware of such extraordinary nineteenth-century painters as Repin, Perov, Kramskoi and Surikov and was fascinated by the pre-revolutionary world they portrayed. I remember thinking that perhaps I might see if I could do some post-graduate work on these stunning painters.

After Moscow we went overnight to East Berlin. That was also a revelation. It was much less drab than I had expected and our East German student hosts were at pains to point out the high-minded architecture, which so contrasted with garish West Berlin. And indeed West Berlin, when we crossed through, did look very garish indeed.

Later that summer, I headed again to Greece with Lucilla for more island-hopping, ending up in Corfu. She then went home and I took the ferry to Brindisi and hitch-hiked all the way to Munich with a young man I met on the ferry, overnighting outside Venice in his tent.

Florence, November 1966

On 4 November 1966, the Arno River above Florence burst its banks and the great *Alluvione* began. I remember the shock waves at the Courtauld as the news came in. Thousands of works of art were being drowned. It was unbelievable. What's more, the timing was terrible. Florentines had just stocked up with their heating oil for the winter so the waters were full of oil. Within a short time we lost many of our tutors who rushed to Florence – John Shearman, my immediate tutor, was one.

A Courtauld friend of mine called Richard Haslam had a mini-van. He said that the Victoria and Albert Museum wanted people to take restoration materials to Florence. He was planning to go. I said I would come too and share the driving. We headed off with our wellies and suitable gear and a hygrometer – and other gadgets for measuring moisture – and blotting paper in the back. I don't know the date we left. It took us a couple of days to drive. On arrival, the water in many central areas was still a foot or so deep. We found that hotels were giving free accommodation to helpers.

We turned up to drop our hygrometer at the Limonaia art-works hospital at the Pitti Palace where Lucilla's old teacher, Professor Tintori, was in charge of the restoration effort. But clearly there were already too many helpers there. We visited the Synagogue, which housed Jewish records, including those from Venice going back to when the Jews were expelled. Finally, through the British Consul, Christopher Pirie-Gordon, we found a place to work. The Guicciardini archive was housed in the basement of their palazzo on the Lungarno beside the river. The Contessa Giuliana Guicciardini – who, with her trim tweeds and grey hair, looked straight off a Scottish moor – had dragooned the army into service and had them load the sodden documents into trucks and shipped them to their castello at Poppiano, Montespertoli, just half an hour south-west of Florence. So every morning Richard and I would set off in the mini-van through the magical landscape of a Tuscan autumn – the vines were golden against the cypress trees – to the exquisite fourteenth-century castello.

I have a photo of Richard and me with the countess and the young count, Francesco, working on the billiard table interleaving damp documents to preserve them. I remember a whole day spent on the letters of a seventeenth-century Guicciardini who had been Florentine ambassador to the court of Louis XIV. It was tantalising because you wanted to read it all. Last summer (2019) Alex and I dropped in on the castello. When we rang the doorbell the current contessa let us in but was not that welcoming. They had had a major burglary many years back in the 1990s and it had clearly made her suspicious of strangers. She was probably in her early sixties so had not been part of the family at the time of the floods. When I described what we did she kept contradicting me. When I got home I googled and found Richard Haslam. He had stayed on long after I had left and had kept in touch with the old contessa for years after till she died at a great age. So he could confirm what I remembered and I sent his email to the current contessa to put her straight. In reply I got a delightful letter from her husband, the count, who featured in the photo and remembered me and referred to us helpers as 'angeli'.

Our hotel soon stopped its free accommodation and we relocated to the Villa Ombrellino, where the ancient Violet Trefusis – who I later read about as Vita Sackville-West's mistress with whom she eloped – was putting up more of the volunteers who were streaming in. I must have been there two weeks before getting a ride home with some Courtauld staff. But before I went I had the most brilliant evening at the opera. The Teatro Communale had been flooded and all the costumes, sets and seats in the stalls ruined. But the show must go on! The season was opening on 27 November with Monteverdi's *L'Incoronazione di Poppea*, starring Claudia Parada, Mirto Picchi, Mirella Parutto, Renato Cesari and the great bass Boris Christoff. Local restaurants provided seats for the orchestra and the stalls; the stars were draped in togas made of sheets; agile men held spotlights and the orchestra played with gusto. I was up in the gods surrounded by locals who were singing along in a way that never happens at Covent Garden. When the show was over onto the stage leaped the mayor to congratulate the cast. Florence would revive. This evening was an example of her fortitude, etc., etc. There was not a dry eye in the house.

1967

My last year at the Courtauld took place a lot in Cambridge. I had become enamoured of Nick Jardine, a brilliant philosopher of science two years older than me who became a fellow of King's College Cambridge when we were first together. I had met Nick quite a bit, initially through Simon Perry when he was an undergraduate and then through my rather odd Yorkshire friend John Procope. John was a classicist at King's who would invite me down to events in Cambridge, including tea with Morgan (E. M. Forster). Nick and I must have got together that autumn of 1966. I remember celebrating Nick's fellowship: only fellows were allowed to walk on the huge grass quad in front of King's which spreads before you as you stand on King's Parade and gasp at the stunning buildings with the exquisite chapel on your right. The night of his fellowship, Nick – wearing his gown and togs – leapt into a handstand and walked across the quad on his hands.

Once, when I was staying with Matt Ridley about 20 years ago, a fellow guest, the scientist Graeme Mitchison, asked me what it was like living with someone as brilliant as Nick. Well, the answer is that I really did not understand most of what he did in his work but I did love the way his mind worked and – despite my ignorance of science – I have always enjoyed spending time with scientists. Through Nick I met a lot of them, including Francis Crick, with whom I became a good friend and whose agent I later became.

If you look up Nick on Wikipedia he is now an Emeritus Professor at Cambridge, described as 'a British mathematician, philosopher of science and its history, historian of astronomy and natural history, and amateur mycologist' (that's the science of mushrooms and I do remember foraging for them in France with him). Nick later married the starry academic Lisa Bronowski – daughter of the famous scientist Jacob Bronowski – who as Lisa Jardine would become a good friend of mine.

Nick was living with a group of post-graduates in Grape House in Grantchester, just south of Cambridge. It was a charming nineteenth-century classical house whose shutters on the top floor reminded Nick of Prime Minister Harold Macmillan's droopy eyebrows. Much of my revision for my finals took place in that garden. I did take Nick to Park

Farm once. It was not a success. He had to borrow a suit as all he had
was a black leather jacket and he looked so uncomfortable in what he
considered a very posh set-up.

My father did not really get the point of Nick and was worried that
I might marry him, which certainly was on my mind – my contemporaries did get married younger then. I remember asking Papa what he
thought was wrong with Nick. His answer was not straightforward: 'I
always hoped you would marry Andy Clive.' Andy was a local tweedy
shooting-fishing young man who lived in Nunnington Hall – a National
Trust property – and whose mother I was very fond of. 'But we have
no interests in common,' I said. 'I think you just want me to be safe.' 'I
suppose you are right,' he said. And we both laughed because it was true.
He would instinctively prefer me to settle with a comfortable landed
gent than a brilliant but unfamiliar academic with whom he had little
to discuss. The irony was that Andy Clive, who worked at that time for
Lazard, ended up in prison for using his clients' funds ...

Nick also hung out a lot with some of his contemporaries who were
architectural students, whose degrees went on for much longer than
the usual three years. One was David Crowther, who I liked very much.
His father Geoffrey had been the editor of the *Economist* and had clearly
made some good money as he owned two villas on the Costa Smeralda,
on the northern coast of Sardinia, which was part of an exclusive development financed by a consortium set up by the Aga Khan. That was
where Nick and I spent a happy beach holiday with David and friends,
who included the dazzling and exotic Charlotte Nassim.

After that holiday I did not even pick up my Courtauld degree but
set off for the US.

With my parents, 1948

With my sisters Libby and Bunny, and a hedgehog at Park Farm, Yorkshire

Libby, Bunny and me. Park Farm, about 1963

About 1964–65

Campaigning with my father in the 1964 election

Rudolf Nureyev in London

Lucilla Kingsbury and me at Park Farm, Yorkshire

My mini-skirt

THE U.S. SCENE

The gun-control movement recoils in Congress

BY OUR U.S. STAFF

THE SHOOTING of Robert Kennedy sparked off such a nation-wide protest in favour of strong gun controls that it seemed certain that some legislation would be passed before the adjournment of this Congress. Now it seems that the gun-control men have been moving too fast for the legislature.

The Senate Judiciary Committee last week debated the strongest gun legislation ever proposed in America. The idea was to make the registration of guns and the licensing of their owners compulsory, and prohibit the interstate mail of rifles and shotguns. On June 27, however, the committee decided to postpone further discussions until July 9. This leaves only 18 working days for the Bill to be debated and passed before August 2, when Congress hopes to adjourn.

Senator Joseph Tydings who proposed the Bill for licensing and registration said that supporters of " responsible " gun-control laws " better realise this was a real defeat and chances of passage are substantially weakened." He added that it would be very easy for the opposition " to mount a filibuster or engage in delaying tactics, either in committee or on the floor in the closing weeks of the session."

July 9 is also the deadline date for the House Rules Committee, which decides what Bills are to be debated, to include any more on the agenda. This date can only be shifted for a Bill of great emergency. A spokesman for the committee said it was unlikely that the Registration and Licensing Bill would be considered in this category. Its only hope would be if it was included as an amendment to the Mail Order Bill which has already passed through the Rules Committee.

President Johnson's Bill well received

Immediately after Robert Kennedy's death, Senator Dodd's Bill banning interstate mail of all firearms except rifles and shotguns was made law. Soon afterwards President Johnson proposed a Bill including rifles and shotguns which was well received. He then decided to make the most of the favourable mood of Congress and called for national registration of all firearms and mandatory licensing of their owners. Senator Tydings' Bill is similar, but says that states should be responsible for registration and licensing, but if after a year they had not acted they would be forced to under Federal law.

Some Senators feel that it was a mistake to try to get a conservative Congress to swallow both the interstate Mail Order Bill and the licensing and registration in one gulp, and they may be right. But proponents of gun legislation are understandably eager to get the Bill passed while gun-control is

still a hot subject, and while there is strong national sympathy for stricter controls. It has become almost an American tradition that in the wake of the assassination of a national figure the country undergoes a period of conscience-searching, and this is the best climate for the legislators to work in.

Their problem is that though opinion polls show the country overwhelmingly in favour of tighter controls—a Harris poll on June 17 found 81 per cent. in support of strong legislation—the

Senator Thomas Dodd

gun-loving minority, led by the National Rifle Association, remains as active a lobbying force as ever, despite Robert Kennedy's death. To the gun lobby, registration would mean the complete abolition of civilian ownership of firearms, and all suggestions of registration have been fought with the lobby's traditional weapon, a storm of letters to Senators and Congressmen.

Such was the outrage at the murder of Robert Kennedy, however, that a counter-storm brewed up. From all over the country, people who normally did not bother with this sort of thing wrote to their Congressmen in support of more control, and this had some interesting effects.

Take the case of Mr. Roman Hruska, a Senator from the hunting state of Nebraska. He was the only man whose previous gun proposals had been backed by the NRA because they would have been so ineffective. He announced that he would back the Bill to ban the interstate sale of rifles and shotguns by post, having only a month before opposed Senator Dodd's milder Bill. He also proposed to keep an open mind on the questions of registration and licensing.

This counter-storm was organised partly by the National Council for a Responsible Firearms Policy, an organisation which, unlike the NRA, is understaffed and short of

money, and works from small offices in north-east Washington. It was the council which took full-page advertisements urging people to write to their Congressmen, and quoting from a speech made by Robert Kennedy: " If we act now, we can save hundreds of lives in this country . . . it is past time that we wipe this stain of violence from our land."

In the last week an offshoot of the council has sprung up: the Emergency Committee for Gun Control, whose chairman is John Glenn, the former astronaut and a close friend of the Kennedys, is staffed mostly by student volunteers. It backs no specific Bill, but supports any that include banning of interstate mail of firearms and licensing and registration. Its purpose is to set up organisations in every state to co-ordinate all independent efforts, and to run a mammoth publicity campaign encouraging people to keep up the pressure of mail on Congress.

Army restricts rifle sales

But even if there is no quick legislation, there have been changes. In the last month several large stores have given up selling guns, including Sears Roebuck and Lechmere Sales—one of New England's largest suppliers of hunting equipment. The Army announced it would no longer support civilian pistol programmes, and would restrict its sales of rifles and ammunition—it was unspecific about the extent of the restrictions.

The nation's airlines have said they will notify the local police at their destination points of any firearm sent by air freight. Several cities have organised campaigns encouraging citizens to hand in their guns, and both Chicago and San Francisco City Boards have made it law that all residents' guns must be registered—in Chicago there is a fine of $500 for failing to register or surrender your gun.

Such localised enthusiasm is of limited import if Congress does not pass its Bill. The Senate Democratic leader, Mr. Mike Mansfield of Montana, and the Republican leader, Mr. Everett Dirksen of Illinois, have both come round to supporting it. But the Democratic leader in the House, Mr. Carl Albert, delivered another blow to its prospects when on July 2 he announced his opposition to all proposed gun control Bills.

If the Bill fails, the issue will be carried into the election campaigns. Those Senators and Congressmen from hunting states and conservative areas who have been won round to supporting legislation may choose to change their views in the face of irate constituents whose votes they wish to woo.

My article on gun control

Travels (from my albums): Anguilla

Travels (from my albums): Southeast Asia

In the US

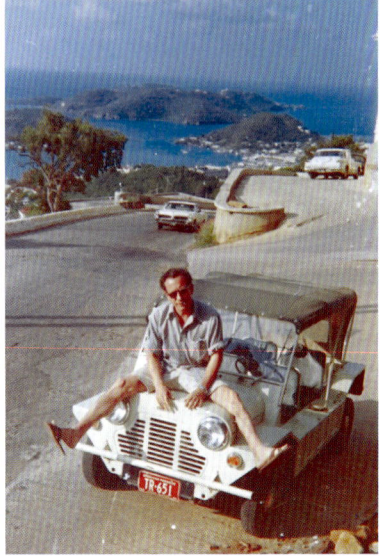

Larry in the Caribbean, 1969

Larry, in about 1969

4.

Discovering America

In July 1967, I hit America for the first time and it embraced me. It was truly love at first sight. I don't remember why I had felt so compelled to go. But certainly for my generation America did seem like the land of opportunity. In the early 60s we were inspired by the glamorous, brilliant young president Jack Kennedy. Any friends I had who had studied in the States were smitten. Nick was not keen on my plans. His was the life of the mind. He would have been entirely happy summering in Grantchester writing away. But I wasn't to be stopped.

Sometime before he died in 2004, my father was 'putting his affairs in order' and handed me a file. In it were my letters from America and – tantalisingly – the carbons of some of those he sent to me. Reading them now brings back the flavour and excitement of it all, if that was needed, for I do remember much of it with the vividness of that intoxicating time.

The cost of flying to New York in 1967 was huge. But there was this brilliant scheme called BUNAC (The British Universities North America Club), which for £50 got you a return ticket to New York, two nights in a hotel and a visa to work for three months. I had no idea how I would work but assumed that waitressing would be my lot.

A few weeks before I left I spent a weekend with my godfather Denis Forman and his wife, Helen, in Essex. I had spent many weekends with the Formans when I was at Kirby Lodge and loved them both. They asked me of my summer plans and I told them. 'Would you like to work in telly?' Denis asked, casually. 'I could ask my friend Ed Sachs.' So he lifted the phone to his friend Ed, who just happened to be a big cheese in CBS TV, and Ed apparently said he would be happy to meet me when I arrived.

So the day after my arrival in Manhattan I found myself in my first skyscraper, making my way to the top, to the lair of Ed Sachs. There he greeted me, rising from his humongous-sized desk with the New York skyline stretching behind him forever. I remember him as warm and wonderfully confident in an all-American way. Googling, I cannot find him and it is entirely possible his name was spelled differently. There were pleasantries about Denis, who he clearly loved. Then he asked what I could do. Well, I had a degree in art history and had worked in a Jermyn Street gallery in London in my spare time making a reference library – a rather grand description of my hours spent cutting pictures out of *Apollo* and *Country Life*.

'Then we might find something for you in the Scenic Design Department – I'll phone Galushi.' Whereupon he did just that, and before long I found myself at the CBS studios at the far west end of West

57th Street meeting the endlessly cheerful Italian-American John Galushi – again, I forget the spelling. Galushi was clearly accustomed to having entitled interns landed on him. There was already a young man called Peter Lieberson, who just happened to be the son of Goddard Lieberson, the president of Columbia Records. Peter was a sweet, rather self-conscious young man just down from college who was not that happy to have me in his space. I later learned that he became a successful composer. Our immediate boss was John Wendell, who became my instant friend.

As I recall, my job was doing quite mundane chores for Wendell and the rest of the time making a useful library of reference pictures for the designers to refer to when creating their sets. Since most of the sets were for contemporary soaps called *Love of Life* (on which I was hooked), *Edge of Night, Secret Storm* and *Love Is a Many Splendored Thing* (which was just about to launch) you might ask what they wanted with Louis XV drawing rooms and rococo candlesticks. The truth was that for most of them this was just the day job. By night and on weekends many worked on shows off Broadway and one wonderfully camp designer called Lloyd Evans, who won an Emmy for his sets for *Love of Life*, actually designed sets for the *Barber of Seville* at New York City Opera at the Lincoln Centre. Lloyd died of AIDS, aged 55, in 1989.

So I had landed in an ambience that suited me just fine. Many days after work a group of us would roll out to the Slate, a bar over the road where a motley group of actors and people from CBS News would hang out. I remember in the bar meeting an Englishman called Thompson who was planning his return home. There would be lots of work in London as he knew how to work with colour – all British channels at the time were black and white.

In one letter, I wrote of feeling 'a bit exhausted as I was out on the tiles last night. My dear boss John organised a marvellous evening. He, his wife, Peter (the boy I work with), another couple and I all went to the theatre to see *America Hurrah*.' After that there was dinner and fascinating clubs in Greenwich Village. 'I am so touched', I wrote, 'by the extreme kindness everyone I work with shows toward me and feel that whenever I go back I shall always have friends here' – which turned out to be the case.

My parents had made a grand trip to America in around 1962. Papa was on the Parliamentary Leader Scheme and was taking in Washington, DC and the East Coast. Mummy joined him with Libby to tour and visit friends in Colorado, Texas and the West Coast, ending in New Orleans. So Mummy's view of America was based on this: its citizens were endlessly welcoming, charming, open, unsophisticated, and insular and strangely naive. My new colleagues at CBS were certainly welcoming and open. But they were as sophisticated and international a group as I could hope for. Many were second-generation Americans and, coming from rural Yorkshire, I was intrigued to know where people's families hailed from. John Wendell's dad was a Pole called Salinsky. On entry at Staten Island he had given his first name, Wendell, to sound more American. 'I always thought I would revert to Salinsky if I took up the violin ...'

Through a friend of a friend I had ended up lodging at 225 East 63rd Street in an apartment with Bonnie Katz. Bonnie worked at IBM as a secretary. She was a warm, friendly person but completely un-interested in the world outside the boroughs of New York. Her mother came in once a week from Queens for supper with her of chicken in soy sauce and – anthropologist-like – I listened, spellbound, to their chatter around New York life. I found Bonnie extremely conventional. She was particularly shocked by my mini dresses – a style that had not yet arrived in NY.

New York in August did not have much ballet to offer but it had concerts and theatre galore and I seem to remember being out most evenings. My Courtauld friend Charles Hope was summering there, working as a computer programmer (he was always scarily clever), and he and I booked for a season of weekly summer concerts together at the Lincoln Centre. It was fun having a person from home to share our reactions to life in the Big Apple with on a regular basis – 'There is so much about America that you want to giggle about, but not in front of Americans,' I wrote.

Mostly my weekends were spent away. I had a 99-day Greyhound bus ticket and visited friends in Princeton, Boston and New Jersey and had a weekend spent largely in the stunning galleries of Philadelphia. I remember being awestruck by a complete medieval cloister uprooted from France and feeling that if the Americans guarded European art so well, they had a right to have it.

Another weekend I went to Washington where Tim Lankester was working at the World Bank. He and Tricia Cockcroft were living in Georgetown, which quite enchanted me. We explored together and I was surprised how much I liked DC. They gave a party for me at which I first met John Graham from the *Financial Times* and Stanley Johnson, who was about the leave the World Bank and had published his first novel – *The Presidential Plot* – of which I bought a signed edition for $5. Stanley wrote his novels on flights – something he continued to do. We visited Stanley and his artist wife Charlotte, who at that point had three small noisy, rambunctious children, one of whom, Alexander, grew up to be the mayor of London and later prime minister.

In early September I took the overnight bus to Montreal where I visited Expo 67. I stayed with Jeremy Baker, an architect friend from London, who was covering the exhibit for magazines so took me round ticket- and queue-free. I was clearly blown away by the exhibition – including the Buckminster Fuller pavilion – and found the whole thing 'an exhilarating experience, beautifully laid out on these islands in the river'. Jeremy was someone who had flourished after leaving London and was saving up to go to Stanford. I wrote back home that it was interesting the way English people seemed to liven up when they crossed the pond.

Then, the two months up, off I headed on 8 September on my cross-America Greyhound. I spent nights on the bus to save time and money and by day I would visit towns where I could see the galleries, Chicago in particular. I was surprised by the thrill of Chicago; by the sheer vibrancy and confidence of the place. I remember the awesome lakeside view of competing skyscrapers and my mini-dress literally blowing up over my head like a reversed umbrella in the famous wind.

No other way would I experience the sheer size of America. I took the northern route. We drove through Iowa, Nebraska, Wyoming and Utah. There was one day when I woke up in Nebraska and went to sleep in Nebraska. Then we went south after Reno and finally arrived at my destination in San Francisco. On Monday, 11 September, I wrote: 'If you have your maps at the ready you will see where I am in Elko, Nevada.' The bus became a companionable place. I got friendly with a mother who was heading to see her hippy daughter in Haight Ashbury, the flower-power centre of San Francisco. I wrote: 'I met many merry students on the bus and some surprisingly interesting elder people. I sat for a long time next to a delightful Argentinian lady whose husband was a professor who had been sent to an American university. So she was taking the chance to see the country by bus – which I thought very game for someone in her mid-fifties.' There were workers and retirees – the medley that was America. But always people were friendly and curious to know about me.

The book that sustained me through much of the journey was Truman Capote's *In Cold Blood*, which was I think the first really successful example of a 'true crime' story following the two murderers of a Midwestern family until they were finally tracked down. The only eerie thing was that those two did seem to keep hopping onto Greyhound buses.

In San Francisco my destination was the University of California at Berkeley where a friend who Tim Lankester had known at Yale was to put me up. I don't remember his name but I do remember having a heavenly time and completely falling for San Francisco. Through another contact I met a beautiful, golden-haired poet who taught in the English department and in this all-too-short romance realised finally that I was not yet ready to settle down with Nick in Grantchester.

Through the poet I met people working for KQED, the independent radio station of San Francisco. For reasons I don't recall, they offered me a job. But of course I would need a green card, which would be complicated. But in all the conversations around it, I realised that America was where I wanted to live now. It was so startlingly more upbeat than England. It was a can-do society in which I felt I could thrive. It was of course novel to people that I was English, so different. But I felt liberated being cut off from the still very class-ridden country I had left and being judged just for myself. I felt that America had transformed me. In my letters I refer several times to thinking of applying for a scholarship – to NYU, Philadelphia, Berkeley, etc. – so clearly I was already set on returning, pronto.

Thanks largely to said poet, I lingered longer than planned in San Francisco and then headed south, skirting LA, and into Arizona and the Grand Canyon, which I shall never forget, then north into Colorado. When we lived in Sowerby Bridge in Yorkshire we had old family friends called Foster – he rather an unexciting man working in textiles and she a sparkling Coloradan called Amorita – with their children, Bruce and Retta. They had emigrated to America when I was about seven and I had missed my naughty best friend Retta. My mother had continued to correspond with Amo and so heard about Retta's progress. She had thrived in Colorado and then gone to Ohio State University in Columbus. It was Amo who greeted me off my bus at Colorado Springs.

Amo was unchanged from my childhood where she had been even more exuberant than my mother. She beamed warmth and welcome and was no doubt happy to be with a childhood friend of Retta. Now she took me under her wing, proudly showing off her spell-binding state, which did seem like God's own country. We went on a trip to Aspen, just when the leaves of the Aspen trees were turning. Against the Rocky Mountains their leaves sparkled like gold. Back in England when I was asked where in America I felt I could most happily live I remember saying Colorado.

Then it was a flight back to New York. I have a picture of John Wendell taking me up the Empire State Building. A New Yorker, he had never been before. And then I flew home. It was early October. It had been three months. But they were months that had genuinely changed my life. The world seemed so much larger, so much more full of possibilities. The job I was returning to on the *Burlington Magazine* now seemed very limiting. I was not looking forward to a reunion with Nick. When I left we had talked about me moving to live with him in Grantchester; we had assumed we would be married. Now I knew that would not work. I just knew he would not be that interested in hearing of my adventures and would resent the fact that I had not kept well in touch.

My return home was as I feared. Nick and I parted sadly and my job on the *Burlington* turned out to be dull. I was the assistant to Ben Nicolson, the editor of the magazine. He was the son of Harold Nicolson and Vita Sackville-West, and clearly his bizarre upbringing at Sissinghurst with his mother dashing off with Violet Trefusis and Virginia Woolf and his father away a lot had not produced a person who was easy in his skin. He was a very sweet man, but shy and clearly entirely uninterested in me.

My job was mostly to type his letters and do a touch of copy-editing. Our office was part of the Thomson empire, situated in a building the wrong end of the Gray's Inn Road surrounded by trade magazines. Ben would head off to lunch – usually at Bianchi's in Frith Street – every day, returning quite late, and I would be alone with Mr Norsworthy, who ran the business of the magazine. Sometimes colourful people, such as Roy Strong from the National Portrait Gallery, would come in with their copy, but mostly there were no diversions and I would slope off down to *The Times* building canteen rather hoping I might meet more stimulating people there – but no such luck.

I still had a lively social life – my diary shows me going to the theatre with Thalia Myers and her husband, Bill, and going to Covent Garden. I was living, as before, in the basement at 153 Gloucester Place with

Caroline. I remember feeling that now I was not in a 'learning situation' I was really worried that my brain would deteriorate. I started systematically reading improving books, including most of Churchill's A *History of the English-Speaking Peoples*, to fend this off. And of course I plotted my return to the US.

It was Tricia who triggered it. Living in Washington, she had done some work for Joe Rogaly, the chief US correspondent for the FT. She said that if I worked for a UK company I would not need a green card. So I wrote off to several Washington correspondents of British newspapers asking if they wanted an assistant for election year. Henry Brandon from the *Sunday Times* got back to me. There would be a job but I would basically be typing, filing, etc. with no chance to write. Then, when I had riskily given notice to Ben Nicolson, Joe Rogaly phoned me in my damp basement and asked me if I could be in Washington in two weeks' time.

I can remember the conversation – on a very crackly, expensive transatlantic line – quite vividly. I asked him what he would pay me. He said $100 a week. I said I had lived in the US and that was not enough to manage on. Would I have the chance to write? He said, 'We have to fill a page every day. Your job is looking after me. But if you write stuff in your own time we would pay you freelance for features at $100 for 1,000 words.' So I was on.

That weekend I went to Yorkshire. Mummy and Daddy were thrilled for me. Mummy was very well at that time. Of course they would pay the fare. What an opportunity! Then Mardy came into the room and Betty told her my news. 'But you can't go to Washington, my dear,' she said. 'It is on fire.' It was 4 April 1968 and Martin Luther King Jr had been shot.

5.

Washington, DC

Years later in 2013, when I was writing my tribute for his funeral, I looked up Joe Rogaly's coverage of the death of Martin Luther King Jr. This is what I read to the congregation:

'There are times when we must pause,' wrote Joe on 5 April 1968. *'This is one of them. We must pause and think for at least a moment about the death of a single individual. A black American who devoted his life to what often seems to be that most hopeless of causes: the eradication of racial hatred.*

'With the death of Dr Martin Luther King, America has lost one of the remaining men of stature who preached love of the white man as earnestly as he preached the advancement of the black man.'

Thus began the first 'thought piece' I read by Joe tucked in on page 13 of the *Financial Times*. Of course he also had the page-one banner headline with President Johnson ordering hundreds of federal troops to quell looting and arson in Washington, cancelling his trip to peace talks on Vietnam and addressing the nation on TV. This was Joe, the agile reporter, telling the story in such a compelling narrative that you raced to the next paragraph. But it was his features when – at the flick of a switch – he changed gear and delivered the most original, thought-provoking, almost confiding thousand words, which I relished.

By Monday Joe has the headline again with more violence, curfews in New York and Washington, and then turn to page 10 by the leader and there are 1,500 words entitled 'A Walk Through Washington', starting:

> America has been brought to its knees this weekend. It is most extraordinary to sit here in the capital of the most powerful nation the world has known and feel the sense of weakness, of hopelessness and of fear, that is all around us.

He describes his neighbourhood silent under curfew, the blackened shops down town. The big shock, the difference from anything before, is that 'This is the revered nation's capital.' He writes:

> I do try to avoid exaggeration in reports but it is hard to talk in soft terms about what is going on in America now. Consider the extraordinary history of the past month, when everything has seemed to fall to pieces at once.

The President has been forced to abdicate from the Government of a divided nation. He seems about to change the course of a war in Asia that America has been fighting with apparent cast-iron determination and the loss of many lives for three years, and he seems ready to make the change because he has been forced by circumstances so to do. On top of this has come the murder of Dr Martin Luther King …

Tricia Lankester, who worked with Joe, describes the day Dr King was shot.

We were all fiddling about in the office in a trivial way, gossiping, and the news came through. Joe jumped as if he'd been given an electric shock. Furious activity and orders to me. Racing. He started writing 'Washington is in flames …' and I pointed out that through the windows it certainly wasn't. 'But it will be in a minute,' he insisted, and then he and I walked to Georgetown since there were no buses, there was smoke coming from 14th street, and you truly hadn't a clue what might happen next. He was utterly focused, calm, waiting, thinking, determined to be ahead of the game on the story but also appalled by what had happened.

On 21 April I landed in a still-smoking Washington and Joe became my boss. I was 22. Joe, the Bureau Chief, was 32.

Washington was a life-changing two years for me. For many people their time at university is when they make their friends for life, transplanted as they are from home to a campus situation. Washington was my campus. I feel I grew up very fast there, surrounded by people who fascinated me and from whom I could learn so much. And they were almost all quite a lot older than me.

On arrival I stayed with the Lankesters in Georgetown. But they were off soon – I don't remember where – and had lent their charming little house to someone else. So I was in a hurry to find somewhere. A few evenings after my arrival Joe took me to a drinks party after work at the house of John Midgley in Cleveland Park. John was the Economist correspondent and I think the party was for some visiting journalist. John, I was to learn, was boundlessly hospitable and would pick up any excuse for a party. I told him that I was looking for somewhere to live. Might his secretary know someone who wanted to share a flat? 'Do you mind basements?' said John in his deep, confiding voice. Whereupon he led me downstairs to a rather dark, wood-lined basement stretching the width of the house. It had all I needed: a bathroom with a little shower, a tiny kitchen and lots of space. I could try it out, he said. I was to have it as my base for the next two years.

John became a father figure to me. We had Yorkshire in common – Midgley is a village in the West Riding. He came from quite a humble background but had thrived at school in Manchester and gone to Cambridge and then got his first job back home on the *Manchester Guardian*. Then in the war he had been in Intelligence and stayed on in Germany after the war to help in reconstruction. This had led to a lifetime interest in Germany and German culture. He had worked for *The Times* in Germany and had then spent many years at the *Economist*. He was sidelined for the job of foreign editor under Geoffrey Crowther and given Washington as a sop. It was the best thing that happened to him. He adored America and thrived there. His contacts and friends were extraordinary. He wrote beautifully and very precisely and I was sad he never wrote a book.

Unfortunately I don't have my letters home from this time. But I do have carbons of my father's letters dictated to his secretary, which comment on the people I told him I had met. He wrote: 'Mardy is worried that once again you have inevitably sunk into a basement but your landlord sounds a better man than Mr Goldfine and Mardy is almost persuaded that it may not be quite so damp as 153 Gloucester Place. To have got a car for the summer too is almost too good to be true. But the best news of all is that you are enjoying the job and as long as you survive it, it could surely hardly be more interesting, educative and I should think would qualify you for anything.' He goes on: 'Mama is still in hospital and after a ghastly period of mass letter writing seems to be very much better and I only hope they keep her there for a good long time whilst Mardy recovers.' I mention this now because I had thought twice about taking the job because I felt I should be around to support my father. But he had so encouraged me to go.

His letters remind me of the people I met with John. Henry Fairlie was a highly regarded British political journalist who was famous for having penned the term 'the Establishment' when describing British political life. My father wrote of him: 'His stock in London was very high. I would say the top political writer when he was in action on the *Daily Mail*. He was gay, hard-drinking, unpredictable but I think well liked. All journalists seem to be hard drinking. How's your drinking?' Henry had clearly had some scandal in London and had gone to the US to start again. He wrote a column for some UK paper and had a long and not-so-public affair with Polly Kraft, the beautiful painter wife of the columnist Joe Kraft. Henry was very much part of John's late-night drinking parties – and very entertaining.

So was Howard Higman – a larger-than-life professor of sociology from Boulder, Colorado. He had found Boulder rather provincial on arrival and so had founded an annual gathering called the Conference of World Affairs that took place every spring. It was an extraordinary event to which writers and all kinds of political thinkers, playwrights, feminists, visionary architects, etc. would all converge. I went in the mid-70s with my then husband Alasdair and it was thrilling. Anyway, John was a regular, as were many British journalists such as Fairlie and David Watt.

Howard was heavily involved in the Peace Corps in Colorado and so had to visit its headquarters in Washington regularly. He always stayed with John and they always gave parties. I can see them together over a hot stove, gloriously happy like the Odd Couple. Howard could be very aggressive when holding forth his views. I once asked him what he so loved about cooking. 'It's the terminology,' he said. 'Crush the garlic, beat the egg, stuff the chicken, whip the cream, chop the beef, etc. ...'

John had been famous for his womanising. He had married young and produced a boy called Steven, a little older than me. But that had not lasted. Then he had married Tanya, an artist, but she could not take Washington. So he was theoretically on his own – nobody could believe he was not groping me ... In fact, he was having a passionate clandestine affair with Elizabeth Farmer. Elizabeth had been known in DC as the very upright, intellectual wife of the lawyer Tom Farmer. I think they had both met at Harvard. She had worked for the famous columnist Walter Lippman. She had a boy aged 13 and twin girls aged 11. She was of German stock in Wisconsin and that had been a link when she met John at a dinner.

It was passion at first sight. There followed several years when their affair continued. She moved out of her house and Tom fought for custody of the children. I don't remember the details but I do remember that we knew that detectives were watching John's house. They were trying to prove that John led a dissolute life and so would not be an appropriate step-father to Elizabeth's children. The case dragged on. Some years later, when I was back in London, John sent me an extract from the detective's report: 'Small blond woman was seen to emerge from the basement and got into a beat up mini car and headed in the direction of the down town area. She stopped to shop at Woodward and Lowthrop where Detective x lost her.'

Anyway, on the rare occasions that I met Elizabeth I got to really love her. People who had known her before were amazed by the transform-ation. She suddenly had a brilliant sense of humour. John brought out the twinkle in her and he was clearly the great passion of her life. At over six feet tall with short red hair, she towered over him and they could not keep their hands off each other. Later they did get married and genuinely lived happily ever after – though arguing a lot, which they both relished.

John and Joe – having been on the *Economist* together – were very close and together they encouraged me. 'What are you working on now?' John would ask and would often give me suggestions. Under my bed I have unearthed the 36,000-word features that I wrote in my own time while working for the FT. There are also lots of news pieces in which – when it seemed incongruous for me to be an authority on the Balance of Payments figures – I appear as 'Our US Staff'. I can't quite believe my 22-/23-year-old confidence.

To begin with I was 'Our US Staff'. Then after nine months I got a by-line. My early features are on unexciting subjects that neither Joe or John Graham would want to touch, like US tourism, US trade with Japan, and then I became an expert on polling and got quite close with Mr Gallup of Gallup Polls fame who I visited in Princeton. But the most exciting was my piece published on 6 June on the gun laws. I had been working on researching the piece for some time – visiting the National Rifle Association (NRA) DC headquarters of the gun lobby and meeting congressman fighting for gun control. Then early on 5 June Joe phoned me from Los Angeles and woke me up. He was at the hotel where Bobby Kennedy had just been shot. They did not know if he was alive. But I must have my piece ready for the first edition.

I sat down, my head spinning, with my notes beside my Olivetti portable, and wrote my 1,000 words. It was completely exhilarating. I had it in the office by the morning. John Graham read it, made a few suggestions and then I telexed it over to London. My father wrote: 'We are all so thrilled with your "Guns for All" article and I am impossibly boastful about it to my friends! I thought it excellent and cannot get over the topicality of it. You told me you were writing it so when I heard of the Kennedy assassination I thought they would use it, bought the paper and there it was.' Later he wrote that his MP friend Tony Leavey said, 'She writes so well and seems to have knocked up the article between the fruit juice and the cornflakes.' And it was wonderful for me to hear praise for what had clearly become my vocation.

The evening after the assassination I remember going out to supper in a restaurant in a group with Tony and Carol Howard and the visiting MP Humphrey Berkeley. I found him pompous and maybe he found me too big for my boots. And I realised later that for the first time I had had the experience that many reporters on the front line get. You are so caught up in the story that you don't quite take in what has really happened. It was only that night when, rather drunk, I got home that I sat and cried about Bobby's death.

That summer was extraordinarily exciting. In May the Poor People's March, planned by Martin Luther King before his death, arrived in Washington led by Ralph Abernathy. Thousands camped out in orderly tents on the Washington Mall. It was called Resurrection City. I remember going down there with Peter Jenkins from the *Guardian* and hearing an incredibly impressive, good-looking young pastor orating. He was called Jesse Jackson.

There was the big build-up to the conventions in August. David Watt – who had been Joe's predecessor in Washington and was now the political editor – arrived to help with coverage. This was not popular with Joe, but he and Susan gave a welcome party – catered by me as cooking nibbles for parties was another side-line of mine – at their home in Cleveland Park. David had been a major success in DC and so some very high-profile people turned up. I remember making friends with Geoffrey Bell, the brilliant economics guru at the British Embassy, who became my lifeline when alone in the office I had to cover matters on the US economy.

I had wanted to go to the Democratic convention in Chicago. But David Palmer was covering that with his assistant Patti. So I got the

Republicans in Miami instead. Joe, John, David and I were going. John was also bringing his Ethiopian girlfriend, Hilary. Joe and I went early and settled in a flash hotel on the front. I remember the first evening Joe taking me out to a Jewish restaurant where he introduced me to the fare he had been brought up on, which included gefilte fish, chicken soup, etc. That's when he talked to me about his Jewish childhood in South Africa where the Rogalys had come to from Eastern Europe via London's East End. Joe's father had been a travelling salesman and had got custody of Joe in his divorce from Joe's mother. Joe had moved from school to school but ended up in Johannesburg and got into Wits University. There he worked nights on the *Rand Daily Mail* with his lifetime friend Ray Heard and on graduation worked for the *Financial Mail*. It was through his boss at the *Financial Mail* that he had made it to the *Economist* in London.

Joe and I became great friends and it lasted till his death in his seventies. But in those early days he was quite possessive of me. He did not like the fact that David Watt and I got on so well and as the summer passed it was clear we were more than just friends. I was very smitten with David and we did have some glorious times together in Washington and in New York – where he introduced me to the joys of the Algonquin Hotel.

The Republican Convention was a complete eye-opener to me. I have never been to a convention since. We were staying next door to the hotel where Nelson Rockefeller and his team were settled and he seemed the most appealing of the candidates to me. But it was Nixon who won the delegates and the full hullabaloo of his acceptance speech had to be seen to be believed. Once the convention was over I came back by train as I longed to see a bit of the 'Old South'. I stayed in a hostel in Charleston and was taken about by a young man who I guess I must have met on the train. He took me to see amazing antebellum houses in the countryside with avenues of trees with moss hanging from their branches – a real caricature of the South. To top it all he took me to see *Gone with the Wind.*

Back in Washington, Midgley had been offered a very grand house in Georgetown for the summer. This was convenient as Andrew Knight, his newly arrived number two who was living in the top of the house, was expecting his wife, Victoria Brittain, and their baby son, Casimir, to arrive. Victoria impressed me a lot. She was very beautiful, and with her almost transparent mini dresses quite took conventional Washington by storm. Andrew was very good-looking and they were very much regarded as a 'beautiful couple'. They had met as journalists working on the *Investors' Chronicle* and now Victoria was planning to freelance for the *New Statesman*. When Andrew was away covering the election candidates Victoria and I spent a lot of time alone together and became good friends – and still are today.

I had been heavily involved in the anti-war movement and had taken part in the march in Washington, getting tear-gassed in the process. I remember talking to David Palmer on the phone the day he and Patti were heading off to Chicago, and Mayor Daly's police were already attacking the anti-war protesters. All David could talk about was what was happening in Prague. I switched on the TV and, sure enough, the Russian tanks were invading. It seemed a strange time that summer to be alive.

In September that year my mother was doing well. She had been in a depression in the summer and Papa had had to cancel a Turkish holiday they had boldly planned. But she was now emerging and so Papa asked their friends Betty and James Cornelius if they could join them on a trip to Marbella. It was a great success. My parents both loved Spain and they had travelled around, swum and had lively times with their friends. One day my mother played a round of golf – something she had not done for many years – and that evening they went dancing. Mummy apparently said that she could not remember when she had been happier. Next morning she was found dead in the swimming pool of the Marbella Club. There was no post-mortem and it was assumed that she had a heart attack. She had had a number of blood transfusions in the past, so no doubt her heart was not that good. She was only 51. I got a call from my father. My mother was dead and he was burying her in Spain as she had been so happy there. He did not encourage me to come home.

Joe gave me the afternoon off and I went with Tricia to the cinema. I said it didn't feel right not to go home and she agreed. So back I went. In Yorkshire Libby and Granny and Pa and I had a little service in our local Mission Room in Sawdon taken by the Rev. Wrigley. He had known my mother well with all her ups and downs, and I remember him saying that he was 'a better man for having known Betty Bryan'. I was particularly moved by that and was glad I had come home. The sad thing was that Bunny was not there. She was working in a kibbutz in Israel. There was no way to contact her – which seems so strange today – and it was another week before she knew.

My return home was timely as I was able to accompany my father to the Tory Party Conference – quite a fun event since I now knew so many journalists and also David Watt was there and we shared lodgings. I became aware that my father was going to be very lonely. My mother's care had occupied him so fully for the last eight agonising years. But now she no longer needed him it left a huge hole. I was living abroad, Libby was off to work in Australia and I really worried for him. I encouraged him to come and visit me in America.

My letters home tell of plans to go to Mexico at Christmas. But that was because I planned to go with David. But in November he wrote to say that he was marrying his long-time girlfriend, Susan. I was devastated and cried my heart out to Midgley. He was quite worldly about it all and was not surprised when I turned up with a new young man who rather fascinated me.

Recently, when I read *Hillbilly Elegy*, I realised that the narrator's background was very much the same as that of Edward, the young man I met and had a coffee with at a Georgetown newspaper stall one lonely Sunday morning. He was charming, good-looking and had the southern drawl of a West Virginian. He came from a poor mining town and had joined the marines to get away. This meant that he was able to go to Ohio State University on the GI Bill, which gave free higher education. Now he was working in some government department and doing well. We connected immediately, and his background was a whole other world. We went out a bit and then he invited me to come with him for a weekend in Columbus to watch Ohio State play Michigan in the big college game. This – my envious friends told me – was a major deal. These Midwestern college teams were tip-top and under their coach Woody Hayes the Ohio State Buckeyes were famously good. The winner of this match would go to the finals at the Rose Bowl in Pasadena, California.

So off I went on Friday, 22 November. Surprisingly, I knew the rules of American football as I had met an American in London from the US Embassy called Coleman J. Parrott who had often invited me to see the film of the latest big game shown every Friday in the US Embassy basement. It was conveniently close to the Courtauld, so eating burgers with Coleman on regular Fridays I had learned enough not to be completely ignorant of the Green Bay Packers and the San Francisco Giants.

My weekend was spectacular. Columbus was very impressive, and many of Edward's old college friends had returned for the game. So it was great fun. The actual game – with all the palaver of the singing and dancing before and in the interval – was a total treat. The home team won and the crowd of over 85,000 went wild. Once it was over fans rushed onto the pitch and to my surprise began to pull down the goalposts. That evening the whole town was in celebration. We watched hundreds of students marching up to the state capitol building holding high the goalposts and chanting, 'We're not afraid of O. J. Simpson! We're for OHIO!!' Who, I asked, was O. J. Simpson? He was a 'running back' and the hero of the University of Southern California (USC) team who Ohio State would meet at the Rose Bowl on New Year's Day. So that was when I first heard of O. J. Simpson – and USC won the game.

My hillbilly romance did not last long. I spent Christmas with some friends in Princeton and in January Papa came to visit me and conveniently coincided with Nixon's inauguration on 20 January. It was really lovely for me to be able to introduce Papa to my friends. He stayed in Midgley's spare room and of course Midgley gave a party for him. He was clearly very impressed with Joe. He came to the office and we watched the inauguration parade from our office windows as fresh-faced young Republicans sang on a float an anodyne song called 'Up With People'. I think Pa went away feeling that I had landed on my feet and was in good hands.

My visit to Charleston had whetted my appetite for things southern – which was lucky as neither John nor Joe had much interest in heading South. Early in 1969 I met a sparkling young lawyer from Atlanta called Wyche Fowler. He had been a postgraduate student at LSE and had made many British friends. I met him in Washington with Andrew Knight and Stephen Fay who was out from the *Sunday Times*. Stephen was heading off to stay with Wyche in Atlanta and they invited me to join them. I asked Joe if I could linger longer than a weekend and perhaps do a piece on the giant Lockheed C5A aircraft, which was made near Atlanta and was the subject of major debate in the Congress on account of its sky-rocketing costs. Joe agreed and I had my first visit to Atlanta.

Wyche was a wonderful host. I remember mint juleps being a speciality. He had a fiancée, Donna, who was a classic southern belle with heavy make-up and hair lacquered to a crisp. She seemed humour free, whereas Wyche was one of the funniest men I had met. I adored his southern drawl and his twinkle. He married the belle and had a daughter, Katherine. But it did not last. In years to come I was to visit Wyche again in Atlanta and also meet up in London and later Oxford, where he taught for a while. He became a congressman for a safe Democrat seat in Atlanta and then risked running for the much less safe Senate seat. He became one of the two senators for Georgia, and once I took my six-year-old Alice to lunch with him in the Senate Dining Room, where he treated her like a princess. However, he lost his Senate seat under Reagan. He then became Clinton's ambassador to Saudi Arabia and we once bumped into each other by chance in the British Airways First-Class Lounge at Heathrow (I was using Alex's air miles) – always we have picked up where we left off.

6.

America 1969–70 and Larry

L aurence Stern, a reporter on the *Washington Post*, and I got together in early 1969. I had met him at various events in the journalists' swim the previous year and knew he was liked and admired by Midgley and was great friends with the British journalist Godfrey Hodgson. But it was at a party some Friday in January that he and I fell for each other and I remember waking up the next morning in his makeshift apartment and feeling very content and also excited.

Larry was not a particularly good-looking man, but it was when he talked and laughed that suddenly his wit and twinkle made him incredibly attractive. Women loved Larry, as I was to learn. He was Jewish

– though not practising – and through him I learned a lot about Jewish humour, and I remember him reading aloud to me in bed the first copy of *Portnoy's Complaint* by Philip Roth – which had caused a sensation on publication in January that year.

The first thing to know about Larry was that he was brilliant and had an extraordinarily subtle understanding of how people and the political system worked. I loved listening to his analysis of the morning's papers. The second thing to know was that he was chaotic. Looking for Larry's keys, his notes, his tickets was a perennial activity. And the third was that he was a lot older than me – by 17 years – and carried considerable baggage as a result.

Larry had married when he got a fellow student pregnant at the University of Missouri. They had one child and then had twins not long after. Then, as an attempt no doubt to keep the marriage together, he had had a fourth child. They had divorced a couple of years back. His wife had kept the family home in North Washington and Larry saw his children – Gunther, aged 16, Cathy and Marc, aged 15, and Christopher, aged 6 – at weekends. So not long after we got together I was embroiled with these kids – who I liked a lot. There were also various former girl-friends whose presence I became aware of – including Joan Bingham, a very beautiful woman whose husband, from the wealthy Kentucky newspaper family, had been tragically killed when a surfboard hit his head as he drove along with his family in the car. Joan later became a very good friend of mine in publishing.

Very soon after we got together Larry found a wonderful duplex apartment in Hillier Place, just round the corner from Dupont Circle. It was light and spacious and that was where I moved in February. Midgley still let me keep my basement, which was handy. In early January the ancient red Mini I had been lent had conked out on a road deep in Virginia during a snow storm, its engine bursting into flame as the oil ran out. And I remember feeling a touch guilty as I used my previous boyfriend Robert's Volkswagen – lent in his absence covering a story for the *Wall Street Journal* – to take my possessions to Hillier Place. Joe was particularly amused by the number of people in my life ('Is it *Newsweek* or the *Washington Post* this evening?') but now I was settling down.

In March we decided to take a holiday. We planned on the US Virgin Islands and on short notice headed off – I remember contrasting the travellers at Dulles Airport: the sporty and lithe heading to Colorado to ski and us slobs heading off to the sun. We arrived in St Thomas, settled into a charming clapboard hotel and rented a little open-topped jeep to tour the island. I have pictures of Larry on the jeep and me on the beach.

But it did not remain peaceful for long. One evening in the hotel bar we overheard the hot news: the Brits had invaded Anguilla. Anguilla is a small island, a former British colony in the Eastern Leeward Islands, which had been run with St Kitts and Nevis. But the Anguillans disliked the rule of St Kitts and – under their local leader, Mr Webster – had declared independence. The British had sent an envoy to sort things out. He was told to leave. On 19 March a contingent of British Parachute Regiment and 40 Metropolitan Police officers peacefully landed on the island, ostensibly to 'restore order' – the police dressed in winter woollies as their summer gear had dropped into the sea.

Larry was immediately on the phone to his news desk. He was on the spot and would of course have to cover the action. I phoned Joe in

Washington but – after a long pause for response from London – was told it was too dangerous to go. So off went Larry. But by day two it was clear that this was a farcical operation and was certainly not that dangerous. So I headed off to Anguilla – along with half the British press corps – to cover the strange events.

I remember back in Washington describing our adventures to Kevin Buckley of *Newsweek*, who immediately sent me a copy of Evelyn Waugh's *Scoop*, such did it resonate. For a start Anguilla had no phone system. So to file our stories we reporters had to hitch what lifts we could off the island. As Larry and I were filing our copy into different time zones, we flew out on different flights. I remember a night in Antigua where I got a lift back with the Air Force and one in Nevis where I got a lift with an eccentric Maltese hotelier called Mary Pomeroy in her tiny private plane, which she named 'the broomstick'. I later learned that she was famous for her terrifying flying and in 1999 she was to head off on 'the broomstick' never to be seen again. Having fallen out with Mr Bradshaw, Mary was relocating to St Martin, busily starting a new hotel called Mary's Boon. Mary was a great addition to our Anguillan visit.

Nick Harman – who was covering the events for the *Sunday Times* – remembers that when a cloud of dust rose from the sandy airstrip it heralded the arrival of a VIP come to negotiate with Mr Webster. One day the press corps chased the sand storm only to find that the VIP walking down the steps of the Lockheed C130 was myself in a pink and yellow sun dress escorted by a para.

The whole escapade appealed to Larry's sense of the ridiculous. Once calm had been established we continued our holiday. But by now we had made a number of friends, including an enchanting man called

Henry Howard and his lady friend Berkley. Henry was an aristocrat from a Catholic Cumbrian family who had been in the Somaliland Camel Corps in the Second World War and had then entered the Colonial Service, ending up as the Administrator of St Kitts-Nevis-Anguilla from 1955 to 1966.

There was something buccaneering about Henry. I don't know at what point he had split up with the mother of his five children and had fallen for Berkley, a charming woman from St Kitts with a lovely soft Caribbean accent. He was in disgrace with his Catholic family and he and Berkley lived happily together on Anguilla. John Graham, who had joined us ostensibly to write a piece for the FT but really to join the fun, got on particularly well with Henry and Berkley and stayed with them on Anguilla another time. I remember seeing Henry looking rather chilly and not at all at home in London. Finally, in 1977 John and I made a pilgrimage to Henry's funeral in Cumbria. We felt we should support Berkley, who had changed her name to Howard by deed poll. It was a bleak affair with all those Catholics in black in the rain. John and I got rather drunk thinking that Henry had lucked out in Anguilla.

Back in DC, I was getting into the swing of Larry's world, much of which revolved around the *Washington Post*, and many of the characters were a generation older than me. His close friends there were Walter and Ann Pincus – he an intellectual reporter from New York and she a very funny, clever, sunny blonde girl from Little Rock, Arkansas, via Vassar College. Larry became godfather to their third child – a daughter named Battle – that year. We spent a lot of time with them. Also Dick Harwood, a rather grumpy man with whom Larry for a while wrote a column. He disliked glamorous Washington but had been smitten by

Bobby Kennedy and spent a lot of time with widow Ethel out at Hickory Hill, tolerated by his sweet wife, Bea.

There was eccentric and provocative Nick Von Hoffman from Chicago, where he had worked in urban programmes with social activist Saul Alinsky and was thick with the likes of Studs Terkel. There was Phil Carter, a dark, curly-haired, exuberant but sometimes brooding southerner from a newspaper-owning family of the *Delta Democrat-Times*, of Greenville, Mississippi, which his brother Hodding Carter then ran. There were Lee Lescaze and his sweet wife, Becky, who had been Larry's assistant on the *Post* when she paired up with Lee. They had two small girls, and Larry was very fond – indeed protective – of Becky. And there was the exuberant Bob Maynard, a black reporter who had dropped out of college but had later been to Harvard on a Nieman Fellowship. He had great style and was such fun.

There were Ward and Ann Just. He was from a newspaper family in the Midwest and had been the *Post*'s correspondent in Vietnam, after which he had published a book, *To What End*. Ann was a delightful woman of some wealth who already had children from a previous marriage and was mostly tied up in domesticity – as were many of the wives of Larry's friends. It was only later that I learned of Ann's steely intellect when she became a local congresswoman in Vermont.

There was the older, distinguished crowd with the brilliant and incorrigible Ben Bradlee at the helm of the *Post*. He was then married to his second wife, an artist called Toni, and for me featured more at large parties where I would also meet Phil Geyelin and the redoubtable Meg Greenfield, from the editorial heights, and the fascinating Eugene Patterson, who had been lured by Ben from being the editor of the liberal *Atlanta Constitution* to be the *Post*'s managing editor. And of course there was Mrs Graham. Katherine Graham, daughter of the previous owner, Eugene Mayer, became the chairman of the *Post* on the suicide of her husband, Philip Graham, in 1963. She was in her early fifties. Larry and she shared a birthday but were not close. I found her quite forbidding, but she and Bradlee clearly were a major team. Her son Don was the heir to the *Post* and Larry later said Don had taken one look at the rather taciturn reporter Len Downie and decided he would be the next editor: there was, said Larry, 'a chromosomal salute'.

There were the younger bunch – Larry was a great encourager of lively aspiring reporters – which included Peter Osnos and his art curator wife, Nina. Nina and I had a lot to talk about on the art front and Peter's enthusiasm was infectious. He had cut his teeth working for the now legendary I. F. Stone, known as Izzy, founder, writer and proprietor, with his tiny wife, Esther, of *I. F. Stone's Weekly*. Peter had worked for two years for Izzy in his family home at 5618 Nebraska Avenue, where Izzy would write the weekly and Esther would type it out, run the circulation and generally manage things sitting in the porch at an ancient typewriter with a sign above it that read 'Good News Is on the Way'. Down in the basement, Peter's first job every morning was to read the *Congressional Record* from front to back, pointing out everything that would be of interest to Izzy.

Izzy had begun his weekly in 1953 out of a sense of frustration at what newspapers chose to publish. In his early days he had changed his name from Isidor Feinstein Stone to I. F. Stone because, with his strong criticism of the activities of the state of Israel and US policy towards it, his then editor did not wish his Jewish name to identify him. His contrarian views also made him an early critic of America's involvement in the Korean War, then Vietnam and South East Asia in general. He said that he never did an interview 'off the record' as he did not believe in getting too close to politicians. He once wrote:

> *I made no claims to 'inside stuff'. I tried to give information which could be documented, so [that] the reader could check it for himself ... Reporters tend to be absorbed by the bureaucracies they cover; they take on the habits, attitudes, and even accents of the military or the diplomatic corps. Should a reporter resist the pressure, there are many ways to get rid of him ... But a reporter covering the whole capital on his own – particularly if he is his own employer [–] is immune from these [political] pressures.*

By the stage in his career when I met Izzy – introduced by Victoria Brittain, who greatly revered him – he was 62. Much of liberal public opinion had by now caught up with Izzy's way of thinking and subscriptions to the *Weekly* – at $5.00 a year – had rocketed to 70,000 with very little increase in expense other than print and postage, making Izzy and Esther prosperous beyond their thrifty dreams.

I remember when they moved to a smart and larger house closer into town on Albemarle Street. Larry took me to their house-warming party – at which Peter Osnos always reminds me I wore a purple *broderie anglaise* dress (home-made) with a matching purple feather boa. *Le tout* radical journalism was there, mingling in the garden with ancient New Deal politicians and friends from the past. I felt honoured to be there.

During my time with Larry, and for long after, I remained very close to Izzy and Esther. But during my Washington time they were a regular feature of our lives. Izzy was fascinated by Britain and followed magazines like the *New Statesman* and *Private Eye* with vigour. I remember them being quite shocked by my steak and kidney pie – offal not being to Washington taste – but being very polite about it.

I meanwhile introduced Larry to British friends who he enjoyed. He was already close with Tony and Carol Howard of the *Observer*. But with me he met Peter and Margaret Jay – Peter, then economics editor of *The Times*, had come over in 1968, along with Margaret, who was covering the election as a producer with *Panorama*. I remember the first time I met Margaret and sort of thinking, 'I want to be you.' With her brilliant job, her great confidence, her good-looking husband and their three children, she seemed to have the perfect life. I remember talking to her about my hopes for my career, which was beginning to take shape, and Margaret saying, 'Of course it's really important to have a career. I go to the office for a rest!' She then elaborated about the chaos and unpredictability of life at home with children as opposed to the more structured and predictable life in the workplace.

I think it was through Margaret that we met Catherine Freeman (also, as Catherine Dove, a former *Panorama* producer) who had come with her husband John, who was the new British ambassador. All the press corps knew about them as John had been a famous TV interviewer on the BBC programme *Face to Face* and had then been editor of the *New Statesman* before being sent by Harold Wilson to be our High Commissioner in India. They made a considerable stir in Washington. With their three young children they were refreshing. Catherine was glamorous in her amazing evening gowns made from Indian saris and with all the wit in the world. I liked her from the start.

Early on Catherine acquired a social secretary in the form of Judith Mitchell and she sort of asked Larry and me to look after Judith. So she would be around a lot. Thus we got invited to many events at the embassy. I remember once being asked at the last minute when some grand lady had dropped out. I always had long dresses that I had made myself and remember turning up in a black-and-white-striped home-made silk dress that evening to find myself next but one to Martha (the mouth) Mitchell, wife of the Attorney General, John. The event was full of grandees and over coffee I spied a rather shy-looking couple sitting alone. I walked up and introduced myself. They were Dick and Barbara Slater, the British ambassador to Cuba and the parents of my friend Guy Slater. We got on really well and they encouraged me to come to Cuba – which I did in December 1969.

1969 is annoyingly the year for which I have no physical appointment diary. I always kept a little one and it must have got lost. So that summer is full of memories of a disconnected sort. I did make a visit back home in June. I remember the excitement of Apollo 11 landing on the moon. That was a Sunday, 20 July, and we were staying at Rehoboth Beach in Maryland, I think with Lee and Becky. It was the same weekend, it turned out, that Teddy Kennedy drove under the bridge connecting Chappaquiddick Island with the mainland, leaving Mary Jo Kopechne drowned in his car. That was a huge scandal when it came to light on that very Sunday of the moon landing.

Larry went up to cover the story for the *Post* and I went with him. We were outside the Court House, Edgartown, on 25 July when Teddy and his glamorous blonde wife Joan appeared. I hadn't been to the coast of New England before. It was both beautiful and quite cold and I remember having to buy a green jersey. When we went to the beach at Cape Cod there was nobody in the sea. I remember running in and finding it as cold as Scarborough back home.

It was that weekend that I gave up smoking. At that point most reporters seemed to smoke. Indeed, I did not feel I could settle down to concentrate on a piece until I had a cigarette in my mouth. I smoked about 40 a day. I don't know what moved me to stop. But I did, just like that. The result was that I put on a lot of weight – Washington drinks parties were awash with cream-based dips, which I gobbled to compensate.

In mid-August there was the excitement of the Woodstock music festival in upstate New York. Not that we were there, but the *Post* and all the media were completely taken up with the event. It was the first of its kind, called 'Three Days of Peace and Music', and around 400,000 young people turned up. The singers included Arlo Guthrie, Janis Joplin, the Grateful Dead, Jimi Hendrix and my heroine Joan Baez.

Late in the summer my sister Bunny visited. She had planned to come to the US in her summer vacation from London University. I was looking forward to hosting her. But instead of coming to Washington she headed straight to San Francisco where she had an introduction to a perfectly wonderful family. She landed, as we say in Yorkshire, with 'her bum in the butter'. The family were called Evers and they were friends of other friends. They lived in a charming wooden house on a hill in San Francisco and the mother ran a lively and homely bookshop. That is where Bun spent much of the summer working. She just loved it. The family loved her and the whole experience was a huge confidence boost for her. America had done the same trick for her as it did for me. She finally did come and stay for a weekend on her way home and we took her to stay with Lee and Becky and their kids near the sea.

The Rogalys were leaving during the summer. I was very sad. Susan had been firm when they came that it would only be for two years. She was very close to her family back in England and in Washington her role was very much the wife and mother – their daughter Rachel was born in 1969. Susan came from a grand banking family, in contrast to Joe, who was socially very insecure and always very aware of it. Her mother, Lady Rose Baring, was very jolly but a lady-in-waiting to the Queen, with all the entitlement that went with that. But it seemed unfair. Joe was on a roll and I was really sad that he had to leave when he was doing so very well and was clearly a star. Joe's role was now taken by John Graham and a new reporter, Jurek Martin, arrived to supplement the office. Jurek was a pro and I liked him.

That summer I became friendly with Sally Quinn. She was a lively and glamorous friend of John Graham and had worked in some capacity at the Algerian Embassy. She described herself as 'an army brat'. Her boyfriend was Warren Hoge: tall, blond and also pretty glamorous, working for the *New York Post*. They were a beautiful couple. I properly got to know her when she joined the *Washington Post*. Ben Bradlee had met her at a party and she had suggested that she could cover parties for the paper – I think that's how it happened. Anyway, she began to do that and also do profiles – I recall her profile of Antonia Fraser when *Mary Queen of Scots* was published. She started doing surprising political profiles in the style section – normally reserved for social coverage

– which caused a stir when she got candid remarks out of the likes of White House stiffs like Haldeman and Erlichman. It became a source of pride to be the subject of one of Sally's often scathing interviews. Sally became very much a part of our lives.

Throughout 1969 the Vietnam War dominated the news agenda. It had brought Lyndon Johnson down and Nixon was determined to come out triumphant with a peace deal. There were many peace demonstrations and I remember that autumn getting tear-gassed in a march on the Mall where things got rough when around 250,0000 people turned up from all over the country to demonstrate. 'We shall overcome,' we sang.

One evening in November Larry was visited at our apartment by a reporter from a small news agency who had an extraordinary story. A reporter called Seymour Hersh had discovered a trial going on of a soldier called William Calley, whose troop was accused of killing over 500 unarmed civilians, including women and children, in a Vietnamese village called My Lai the year before. I remember Larry pacing around the floor in incredulity as the story emerged.

Days later it was the lead in the *New York Times* and the *Post*. It was a turning point for many. Nixon was trying to slow the war down – Vietnamisation was the name of the process as they tried to bring more US soldiers home, replacing them with locals. My Lai told people the story of what actually could go on. It was shocking beyond words and was to lead to even lower morale among troops in the field.

That December I went to Cuba on a short holiday to stay with Dick and Barbara Slater. Getting to Cuba from the US was notoriously tricky, involving expensive visas acquired in Mexico. But the diplomatic flight from the Bahamas sorted that out so I got there easily. On my first evening my hosts were wonderfully warm. But then it emerged that there had been a mistake. I had come for two weeks; they thought I had come for one. They would be leaving after a week. As it turned out, after the initial surprise, this was fine. I went off to a large Havana hotel – occupied, it seemed, largely by Russian engineers – and asked to arrange a tour of the island the following week. This seemed perfectly possible as they were used to entertaining the Russians so I reassured Barbara and Dick that I could look after myself from my base in their residence.

Cuba was fascinating. Dick clearly loved the place. He was a Latin American specialist so it suited him well. He emphasised the bright side – the excellent education system, the healthcare, the poverty that had been relieved under Castro. It was not that long since independence and I remember talking to people in ice-cream queues – one of the main entertainments, which always lasted at least an hour – about life in Cuba before Castro. Because Cuba had been dominated by America under Battista's regime, many people spoke English and I had intriguing conversations. There was no doubt that, for the poor, things had improved hugely. There was a great feeling of pride in their independence.

I asked Dick what he would like his next posting to be. It would be his last. He said he would love Chile. He had worked there before – in fact, if he had landed it he would have been there for the CIA coup that grounded Allende. But while I was there he and Barbara received the news of where they were bound for and were clearly not at all pleased. They were not allowed to tell me, which was difficult for them as they would clearly have liked to discuss it at meals. It later emerged that Dick

– whose speciality was Russia and Latin America and who had never set foot in Africa – was being sent to Uganda. This was the Foreign Office in its silliest 'talented amateur' mode and of course had disastrous results.

My Cuban travels outside Havana were fun. The island is long and thin. I had a guide and a driver and a 1954 black Cadillac and we headed down the spine of the island. It was spellbinding with its striding tall palm trees. We headed south-east to Cienfuegos, then Santa Clara, always staying in rather bleak hotels. I think our final destination was Santiago de Cuba, but long before we got there the Cadillac broke down and we ended up coming back to Havana on a lively but crowded bus. Also, while I was alone in Havana I spent time with Magda Moyano – an Argentinian whose sister Dolores I knew in Washington. She was working with the famous anthropologist Oscar Lewis, who was studying the life of Cuban peasants under Castro's regime. Magda had the extra exotic twist that she had lived as a child and teenager next door to Che Guevara in Buenos Aires.

Back in Washington Larry was there to greet me and I remember spending some of Christmas with John Midgley and spending time with Elizabeth and her 13-year-old red-haired twins who – now that Elizabeth was being more public about her relationship – became a feature of my life.

7.

1970 Travels

Early in 1970 I was offered a job on the *Economist* back in London, writing for the American Survey. I don't remember how it happened. I had met Nancy Balfour, the strong-minded dynamo who ran the American Survey, through John Midgley early in my time in Washington. But now, when I had lived there nearly two years and was well settled in, the offer was made.

I know I was torn. My job on the FT had gone really well. I loved Washington. From a standing start I now had regular features in the paper every two weeks with my own by-line and was covering US news as 'Our US Staff'. It had been a fantastic break for me. On the other hand, I was still technically the locally hired assistant to the US editor working on quite mundane things for him and not a proper journalist. The job I was being offered would be as a full-time journalist on a prestigious paper, which was particularly highly regarded by my friends in the US. In theory it was a no-brainer.

But then there was Larry. We were extraordinarily happy together in our nest in Hillier Place and I was also very tied up with his kids, particularly Cathy. I loved his friends, who had become my friends. But he was 17 years older than me and was clearly wanting to settle down with me. I was 24, ambitious for a career and not ready for that. I had a recurring nightmare of myself in a station wagon in Chevy Chase, Maryland, with a gang of kids. The fact that Larry completely understood my dilemma did not really help. So I took the job and agreed that I would return to London in April. We had less than three months left.

I don't know how long it took. But it seemed like the next day that Larry walked in saying words to the effect of 'If you are off, so am I!' He had been offered the job of bureau chief in Saigon, now known as Ho Chi Minh City – and it started in February. For him it was also a no-brainer. Because of his family situation he had never had the foreign posting that any ambitious young reporter would have liked. At 40, this was an extraordinary opportunity at a time when all eyes were on Vietnam. But they wanted him there pronto. I had the prospect of being left alone in DC. The boot was on the other foot.

Frantic arrangements began. I had saved my 'features money' and could afford the Pan Am around-the-world ticket that cost $1,500 and allowed you to drop off where you liked. I asked John Graham if I could depart in early February, leaving me over two months to come home via Vietnam. He agreed and found my replacement in Sarah Riddell. Suddenly it was very exciting. I am never happier than when reading a map and I traced our journey. I had always wanted to go to the Far East and to Japan – where my father was born. I also got myself a visa for Cambodia and Laos (Americans could not get Cambodian visas) as I was determined to go to Angkor Wat.

Farewells began. I had a particularly moving one with John Midgley. He had never let me pay him rent – just expenses – on my handy basement. I wanted to give him a huge treat. So we spent a magic day – interrupted by a good lunch – buying rare bone china of the design he loved. His old girlfriend Anne Mansfield, daughter of the distinguished Senator Mike Mansfield, had sent me money from London to increase the pot. The antique dealer did not know what had hit him as we binged on porcelain. I was glad to leave John something physical to remember our friendship. He had been the most perfect father figure to me over the two years and I knew we were friends for life.

I have photos of Larry and me at a farewell party thrown for us, I think, by Walter and Ann Pincus. My long hair is piled on my head and I am wearing a purple batik printed Thai silk dress that Larry had bought for me in the Caribbean. I still have it today.

Then on 26 February off we flew westward over the Pole to Japan. The point of stopping our journey in Japan and Hong Kong was for Larry to get to know the local *Washington Post*'s bureau chiefs and be briefed by them. So I was very much left to myself. On our first day in Tokyo it snowed. Not a beautiful snow but a dreary grey snow with lowering clouds. I remember sitting in our bleak hotel room feeling cold and very sad. It was in Japan that it really hit me what I was doing. I was travelling with the man I loved and who I was going to leave and I sank into a depression, which very much colours my memory of my one trip to Japan.

And February is not a good visiting time for Japan. We went out to Kamakura and ate cross-legged in a restaurant looking at exquisite Buddhist shrines. But little could raise my spirits. There seemed to be crowds bustling everywhere – what's more they were all my height, which was novel. But I found the Japanese crowd phenomenon quite oppressive – everything seemed to be done *en groupe* with a flag-holding leader, which was also new to me. The following day I went alone to Kyoto on the bullet train to see the renowned gardens. But outside the gardens Kyoto seemed ugly and shrouded in electric and telephone wires, not to mention smog and cold drizzle. I found the day depressing.

So it was with relief that we left for Hong Kong. I shall never forget Larry's response to the bustle of Hong Kong. Japan had seemed very 'Western' and ordered, but this seemed like the real Far East. Hong Kong markets were amazing. Larry had never seen a dead chicken before unless it was plucked in cling film. The bags of live frogs, the unmentionable innards – in fact, all the food – was also a shock to this all-American man who – except for a short time working on the *Stars and Stripes* in 1947 – had never been abroad before. I simply loved it.

We were welcomed by Stan Karnow, the *Washington Post* correspondent, and his wife, Annette. Stan was a terrific raconteur, who I got to know really well later when I was a literary agent. He was also extremely funny. He went on to write the great definitive book on the Vietnam War. Anyway, Hong Kong cheered me up a lot. We also had a jolly Chinese dinner with Kevin Buckley, the very *Newsweek* correspondent who had sent me *Scoop*. That was the beginning of a great friendship for both Larry and me.

After four days we were off to Saigon. Looking back, I feel so very privileged that I did visit South Vietnam under US management. Nobody could quite describe the scenario that hit us on arrival; the feel of the arrogance of US power in this country despite all the opposition back home. At that time the US had around 340,000 troops in Vietnam. There was no doubt who was in charge. There was also this exotic mix of French post-colonial and Vietnamese life, so wonderfully captured in Graham Greene's *The Quiet American*. And to cap it all, our mammoth, tatty room, with a balcony overlooking the square, was in the Hotel Continental, where Graham Greene wrote his book.

The *Washington Post's* current correspondent was the young and very lively Bob Kaiser. Technically Larry was his boss. But Bob and his wife, Hannah, had been there well over a year and knew the ropes. I was aware that I was not going to be able to do any reporting in Vietnam. I had a deal with the FT that I could send them pieces if I was in a place where there was not an FT correspondent. But the FT had a stringer in Saigon and, what's more, getting registered with the US administration as a member of the press corps was not possible. The press was completely controlled and relied on the army and air force to get them about. It was a classic wartime situation.

But in Laos, next door, this was not the case. And no sooner had we settled into the Continental than Larry decided to go to Laos to do a story on the situation there. We flew to Vientiane, the capital, along with some other press corps. All of Indochina, bar Thailand, had been a French colony. And in Vientiane you got a feel of what Saigon might have been like before the Americans arrived. There was that happy gourmet scene that the French leave behind – unlike the British with their steak pies – and we dined in restaurants run by Frenchmen who had stayed on after independence.

We were also made welcome by the French ambassador – Britain did not have one – who had us to lunch. Everyone I know who has lived in Laos comes away loving the people – and the ambassador was no exception. There is a gentleness about the Lao, which is so totally different from the dynamic, often warlike Vietnamese. Vietnam had dominated the Lao historically and Laotians often made anti-Vietnamese jokes. But the Kingdom of a Million Elephants Under the White Parasol had a proud history.

Many had died in Laos. In this Cold War scenario there were two parties: the Royal Laotian Government, who looked to their leader, Souvanna Phouma, and the guerrilla Communist Pathet Lao, led by his half-brother Prince Souphanouvong and supported by the North Vietnamese and Russia. But all the country revered the king, who resided in Luang Prabang further north. There was civil war in the north and there were regular spats between the two sides. Meanwhile, the Hmong tribespeople in the north had been infiltrated by the CIA – and were to suffer from this after the US went home.

The road north was not safe. So after a couple of days we flew in a tiny plane – the only time I have been shot at – to Luang Prabang. There we became very aware of the Hmong presence. These hill people in the market stores looked completely different from the Lao and – like the Kurds in the Middle East – lived across several countries. Our first evening in Luang Prabang we were waiting in Souphanouvong's garden to hear of a visit from an emissary from Hanoi. Suddenly, in came the Reuters correspondent to tell us that the South Vietnamese Embassy in

Phnom Penh in Cambodia had been sacked. This was a news story and I was the only person with a Cambodian visa.

We flew back to Vientiane and the next day, along with veteran LA *Times* correspondent Keyes Beech, hopped on a plane to Phnom Penh – Larry and Keyes ignoring the immigration officials on arrival. There we settled ourselves in the best hotel in town: the Hotel Royal. Once again we were in French colonial heaven with wide boulevards and glorious markets and none of the US vulgarity and tat of Saigon. Cambodia was an independent country ruled by Prince Sihanouk, who had so far cannily managed to keep his little country out of the war raging on its border. We were driven around town by cyclo. Larry and I both wrote stories about the embassy sacking, met the British ambassador, who seemed as bemused as anyone about what was going on, and then I put Larry on a plane to Saigon, had a lovely pool-side lunch talking about life with wise old Keyes, and then headed on my adventure to Angkor Wat.

My visit to Angkor will remain with me all my life. To get there you joined a 'limo'. These were people-carriers that picked up passengers as they went along. Starting early, I had a good seat and was the only non-local on board. But soon we were filled to bursting as we drove north to Siem Reap. Everyone, it appeared, was heading for Angkor. Why were they going on this day, I asked in my best French? 'Nous allons au "fête funèbre", they replied. It turned out that when the abbot of the monastery died they kept his body for some weeks and then they burned it on a huge bonfire in front of the temple and had a major party. It was just my great luck that I had hit this day.

On arrival in Siem Reap I hailed a cyclo driver and asked him to take me to the Auberges des Temples, the only hotel at Angkor, at which I had made a booking. Dusk had fallen when we arrived and the bonfire was alight – as were flares all around the area in front of the stunning floodlit main temple. And there were thousands of people. The only tourists I spied were a French family who were staying in my hotel. Everyone else had come from miles around. I asked my driver if he could stay with me and be my guide. There were all kinds of entertainments: amazing puppet shows; traditional Cambodian dancers with their temple-like head-dresses and pointy shoes; bands playing music; every kind of food stand. And if you wanted you paid your money and you joined the communal dance – which I did with my sweet driver. The overall atmosphere was one of celebration. All made me so welcome in their mercifully peaceful country. I shall always treasure that. Years later, when Pol Pot laid waste to the land and Kissinger said that when I was there was the height of Communist infiltration into Cambodia, I would not believe him.

For the next two days I had Angkor to myself. My driver cycled me all around the huge area of the main temples and I bought rubbings of the incredible reliefs of gods and dancers on the temple sides – which I have to this day. On the second day we went to the temples at Banteay Srei. What stunned me was the way the tropical jungle was constantly growing through the ancient ruins. I have photos from there, including a moving one of the huge stone bridge with larger-than-life-sized seated stone figures called the Avenue of Giants. There must have been about 60 of them. Later many of their heads were gone, sold on the inter-national art market during Pol Pot's time, but from googling I see that they have been replaced.

Back in Phnom Penh I went to see Charles Meyer, a Frenchman who was a close advisor to Prince Sihanouk, who I had met with his Chinese wife when I first arrived. Sihanouk was away in Paris at the time. I said I was leaving for Saigon and had come to say goodbye. 'Don't go now,' they said. They had tickets for me to watch the Royal Ballet in which Sihanouk's daughter was a lead dancer that night. I said I was sorry but I was expected and had got my air ticket. 'I think you should stay,' said Charles. 'It's beginning to get interesting.' Little did he know. The flight I took out was the last flight before the army coup under Lon Nol that ousted Sihanouk and brought in a new regime that would welcome the Americans.

I was of course furious. If only I had stayed I would have been the only reporter in town to tell the story. As it was, I was kicking my heels in Saigon. Dear Hannah Kaiser took me under her wing, showing me around Saigon. In my diary I see we went to formal dinners and I remember sitting next to Ellsworth Bunker, the hawkish US ambassador. Saigon at night was a shock. There were all these GIs on R&R, many of them huge soldiers, in the bars with the diminutive and beautiful Vietnamese girls wearing their exquisitely elegant dresses called *áo dài*.

Within days Larry and I returned to Laos for a five-day stint, where we learned a great deal. We visited refugee camps in the country-side, where we became so aware of the US infiltration and bombing. Enthusiastic peasants showed us the oil lamps that they made out of cluster bombs. Larry had a CIA friend called Jerry Daniels – a laconic Montanan based in the north, working with the Hmong tribespeople, and I am sure Jerry told Larry more than I ever knew about what they were up to. We hung out with Jerry a lot. He had been trained as a smokejumper (highly trained firefighters who parachute to attack wildland country fires), which, I guess, equipped him for his work in the mountains bringing in supplies to the secret army based around Long Cheng. He wrote crime novels under a pseudonym in his spare time.

Looking up on Wiki now I read that Jerry continued to work as liaison between the CIA and the Hmong and their general Vang Pao. And in 1975, when the North Vietnamese invaded, Jerry 'organised the air evacuation of Vang Pao and more than two thousand of his officers, soldiers, and their families to Thailand. Immediately after the departure of Daniels and Vang Pao, thousands more Hmong fled across the Mekong to Thailand where they lived in refugee camps. From 1975 to 1982 Daniels worked among Hmong refugees in Thailand facilitating the resettlement of more than 50,000 of them in the United States and other countries.' He died a mysterious death in San Francisco in 1982 – which was the subject of an investigative book, *Hog's Exit*. In the Amazon reviews I read:

> No other American is more recognised and beloved to the Hmong than Mr. Jerry Daniels. In the battlefield, he ate and lived the way they did. He took care of them and in return they treated him like a brother. He was one of them.

My other vivid memory of Vientiane was going to my first – and only – brothel. It was a merry-looking place called the White Rose, which I think Jerry took us to along with various other reporters. As we sat at the bar, sweet, innocent-looking young Laotian girls were rushing in and out of the cubicles upstairs. Meanwhile, those not thus occupied did a floor show, where I remember sitting aghast as a plump naked girl did her party piece of smoking a cigarette in her vagina. As she puffed away I was so shocked that I did not know where to look. Larry was also confused by this humiliating spectacle and we left in silence.

Then it was back to Saigon, and on 26 March my diary just says 'to Bangkok'. Goodness knows what was going on in my head.

In Bangkok I stayed with the jolly Michael and Phyllida Wrigley – he from Yorkshire via MI6 – and had drinks with the legendary *Times* journalist Richard Hughes, who was inspiration for Dikko Henderson in the Bond novel *You Only Live Twice* and for Old Craw in le Carré's *The Honourable Schoolboy*. Then on to stay in Kathmandu, which involved driving out in the dark to see the sun rise on Everest. And finally into Delhi.

Tim and Tricia Lankester were my destination – Tim had been sent to India by the World Bank the year before. There was Tricia greeting me in their airy flat in Sundar Nagar, heavily pregnant with what was to be my godchild Alex. They were already clearly smitten with India and had made a fascinating assortment of friends. I loved my stay with them. There were little excursions to the Taj Mahal and the Red Fort. But just wandering around Delhi made me gasp. I could not get over the crowds, the smells and the sheer presence of humanity at its most congested. I remember getting lost in Old Delhi and feeling a genuine panic with all these beggars reaching out to touch me and thinking about Adela's panic in *A Passage to India*.

My memory of India was very much coloured by the plane reading on the journey home. Someone had given me V. S. Naipaul's *An Area of Darkness*. I had never read Naipaul before and was bewitched by his prose. But he is a fastidious man and India had clearly appalled him in many ways. Such was the passion of his writing that I too remembered the piles of excrement and the smell of the crowds quite out of proportion to everything else. It was only when I returned two years later for a proper journey that I got to be truly swept up in that country.

8.

1970 London – the *Economist*

———◇———

M y return to London was a complete change to the life I had
left in 1968. I now had a good job and could afford to live
somewhere comfortable. I had taken off weight in my travels and now
bought elegant clothes as opposed to the home-made ones I had worn
in Washington. I remember buying three smart trouser suits and a
flattering cream cocktail garment and generally feeling that I looked a
professional.

Caroline Ross, my flatmate, had married her boyfriend John Weeks
early in the year. So there was no going back to Gloucester Place. Instead
I stayed upstairs in Gibson Square in the house of Andrew Knight and
Victoria Brittain while looking for somewhere to live.

Thanks to Midgley's generosity I had saved $3,000 in Washington.
Half of it had been spent on my round-the-world Pan Am ticket. I had

planned to rent a flat in London, but soon, looking at Victoria's friends who were all busy doing up houses at cheap prices in Islington, I realised that it was silly to rent and I should spend my savings on a down-payment on a flat. I had retrieved my white Mini – somewhat battered by two years in Bunny's care – so was set and could live less centrally. Many of my friends lived in North London – the Rogalys, David Palmer and Victoria for a start. I worked out that with a mortgage I could afford a £4,000 flat and I began looking in Islington and in Highbury and Tufnell Park.

Then one day I chanced upon an ad for a house in Holloway. This was a rather run-down area between Islington and Tufnell Park but the house, at £4,000, was worth looking at. It turned out that the reason it was so cheap was that there was a sitting tenant in the form of Annie, an elderly woman probably around 80, who lived in the two rooms at the top of the house. The agent told me that with a sitting tenant I would have difficulty getting a commercial mortgage but could apply for one from Islington Council.

Thus it was that I ended up in 18 Mayton Street, N7, a quiet south-facing, three-storey row house of which I occupied two floors. My vendors were a young working-class English couple who were moving, along with many of their friends, to Canvey Island in Essex. My neighbours were mostly Greek Cypriot and Pakistani, and the shops around reflected this. The couple had converted the downstairs from two rooms into one long room with a kitchen and bathroom extension at the end, out of which stretched a long grassy garden. It was the garden that captivated me. I had always been brought up with gardens, my mother being a manic gardener in more ways than one. And the potential of Mayton Street's garden was too good to be true.

It all happened quite fast. I remember the day I moved in. Charlie Morland came with me and was so encouraging. I had room to entertain and, what's more, I had a spare room to have friends to stay in. I felt sort of settled. I have pictures of a housewarming party in my garden with Victoria and Casimir.

Meanwhile, my job was interesting but not as thrilling as I had hoped. Nancy Balfour ran the American Survey in her own systematic way. Long pieces came in from Midgley in Washington and from stringers in New York and California. We in the London office filled all the gaps, providing the week's news from the US. A lot of this was done by reading US papers and magazines. So I missed going out on stories in the way I had in Washington.

But the *Economist* was interesting in itself. At times there was a theatricality about the characters who worked there. Every Monday morning Nancy and her very sweet and competent American sidekick Margaret Cruickshank made a list of likely topics we would cover. Then at 11.00 we trooped into the office of the editor Alastair Burnet along with all the other *Economist* journalists and each head of department – Brian Beedham at Foreign, Mary Goldring in Business, George Fitch in Home, etc. – outlined what they planned to cover that week. Obviously this could change with events, but the bones were laid out there. Alastair always seemed incredibly relaxed and appeared to run the show like a school magazine. He relied heavily on his deputy, Norman Macrae, to provide the intellectual heft for which *Economist* editorials were famous. But politics was clearly Alastair's lifeblood and he also covered it as a regular presenter on ITN's *News at 10* and was responsible for ITN's election coverage.

The *Economist* was interesting in that about half its journalist staff were women, which in 1970 was not the case in Fleet Street. The American Survey was entirely women, including my friend Mary Hughes and Brenda Maddox covering technology. Midgley said that Geoffrey Crowther had been responsible for this when he was editor. He is quoted as saying, 'You can hire a first-rate woman for the price of a second-rate man.' He encouraged women because they tended to be very loyal as there were not many job opportunities for them in Fleet Street. Marjorie Deane, the redoubtable writer on Economics and Banking, of whom I became very fond, stayed there over 40 years. Also on a weekly paper they could combine childcare more easily. One of the most inspiring women – who I at one point shared an office with – was the warm and witty American Emily MacFarquhar, who covered China and was married to an academic China-watcher, Roderick MacFarquhar. The way she talked about combining her work life and her children encouraged me no end.

The internal politics of the *Economist* was pretty fascinating too. I had heard a lot about Brian Beedham from Midgley. Brian had got the foreign editorship instead of John. Brian's defining belief was in the evil of Communism and thus he was a major hawk on Vietnam. This was in opposition to both Nancy Balfour and Midgley and also I think to Barbara Smith, the brilliant, gentle writer on the Middle East. So sometimes there would be conflicting editorials in the front of the paper on foreign policy. Nancy was also often at odds with Mary Goldring. Both of these ladies were fearsome and would have strong disagreements on subjects such as airline policy – Mary had been nicknamed, by some unknown source, as 'Miss Swing Wing'.

That June Harold Wilson, the Labour leader, called an election. To my delight, Alastair said they needed extra journalists to supplement the Home department and so I found myself roaring around Devon after the charming Jeremy Thorpe, then leader of the Liberal Party, and round Essex with the heavy-drinking George Brown, the deputy leader of the Labour Party. On election night the Rogalys gave a party to watch the results come in. Most pundits, including David Watt, had said that Labour under Wilson would be returned. And to our surprise Ted Heath came in with a Tory majority of 30. I had really enjoyed those few weeks reporting and they confirmed that I was not in the right place. I can't remember at what point I moved to the Home department, but certainly within less than a year I had done so.

That summer I was having a lively social life, but I shall return to that after the *Economist*. Looking back on my life I think it is really important that at some time, preferably early on, you have a period when you feel undermined. You feel a failure. Only thus can you empathise with people who feel trapped in a workplace where they cannot be fulfilled. My time in the Home department did not begin well. Perhaps I was too accustomed to being encouraged by Joe and John at the FT. But certainly encouragement was not on the cards now.

George Fitch ran the Home department. He was a lazy man and an old mate of Alastair Burnet. In down times they spent a lot of time watching racing on TV together in Alastair's office. He relied heavily on Sarah Hogg, a very clever, well-connected (her father-in-law was the Tory peer Quintin Hogg, later the Lord Chancellor) young woman who had come there straight from Oxford some years before. She exuded entitlement and was not pleased by my arrival. There was Robert, who covered labour relations and who admitted to me years later that he had felt diminished and elbowed out by Sarah and George. Most of the other staff were women who worked part-time but had very firm beats like Education, Health and Social Services. Many ideas I suggested for pieces at our Monday-morning meeting were firmly sat upon because they involved the fiefs of these ladies.

So my job was to find areas not necessarily well covered and that involved moving around the country. My friend Marietta Procope's boyfriend Fazle Hasan Abed was from East Pakistan. He was a delightful, softly spoken, very clever Bengali who was working as an accountant. Through him I learned of the movement, for an independent Bangladesh and wrote pieces covering their movement, Action Bangladesh. I would spend evenings in Marietta's house in Camden stuffing envelopes with leaflets. This meant that in March 1971 when the military junta in West Pakistan attacked East Pakistan and the war began, eventually involving India, I was quite well informed. I wrote one particular piece from Bradford about how the war was affecting the overall Pakistani community who had previously been united in their efforts to confront the racism they experienced in England but were now from countries technically at war. I remember being pleased that it featured on a radio programme of notable pieces that week.

I also found an ally in Gordon Lee, who ran the *Economist's* Surveys. These were, and still are, lengthy pieces within the paper that can run to around 20,000 words. Gordon suggested I might like to work on the survey they planned on British tourism. It was instigated from the Business department, where a sparky woman was already working on the economics, but they wanted someone who would do more of the colourful stuff, which would involve travelling around the country. I remember having a fascinating time recording the English on holiday – day trips to Clacton, B&Bs in North Wales resorts – and I enjoyed accompanying a group of Americans on their Cotswold run, with Oxford and Stratford as highlights. Between us we produced our 20,000 words and I had my name in the paper for the first time. That was valuable. The problem on the *Economist* was that you were anonymous, which made it difficult looking for jobs elsewhere.

As I recall, it was Gordon who encouraged me in my suggestion that the *Economist* should run a series of Arts briefs. Business briefs were a feature of the paper where a particular area of business was explained over a two-page spread of around 2,000 words. I said that the world of theatre, opera, ballet, art galleries, orchestras, etc., with its mixture of public and private finance and potential for international tourism, would be of interest to our readers. They were also my passions. I think I ended up writing about six Arts briefs. Working on them gave me something to always be doing when work lagged in the Home department and it also gave me the chance to get out of London, exploring provincial theatres and orchestras and regional arts associations. These were the brain children of Jenny Lee, who had been Harold Wilson's inspired first Minister for the Arts, as a way of distributing public money outside London and raising private money for arts projects locally.

I particularly enjoyed working on my brief on the London commercial theatre, which involved meeting wonderfully colourful producer/impresarios like Bernie Delfont – with his huge desk and permanent cigar – Binkie Beaumont and John Gale. Many of their shows were tried out in the provinces first, hitting the West End after a run. I was particularly intrigued by how they financed with a mixture of their own money, other large investors and lots of small investors – known as Angels – who bought a small share and then had the added advantage of encouraging all their friends to come and cheer loudly on the first night.

When I left the *Economist* I wrote to John Gale, a producer who had made huge money with commercial hits like the French farce *Boeing*, Noël Coward's *Present Laughter* and *The Secretary Bird* (capitalised at £8,000, it made £4,000 a week for several years, making his fortune) in the 1960s. John was an interesting, amusing man: a product of Christ's Hospital School where the arts were encouraged, he trained and worked for ten years as an actor in the provinces and London so knew theatre inside out and was married to an actress. Though his tastes were quite highbrow – he ran Chichester Theatre in the late 80s – he had an instinct for 'quality commercial'. I asked him if I could be put on his Angel list. The first one I was offered was *No Sex Please, We're British*. I rather snootily turned this down and thus missed out on a huge hit, which ran at three different West End theatres from 1971–87. The next I was offered was *Lloyd George Knew my Father*, a comedy by William Douglas Home. I put £200 up and made about £2,500, which paid for the conversion of my loft in Mayton Street.

My second survey for the *Economist* in summer 1972 was on Wales. I had spent time in Wales as a child, holidaying regularly in Snowdonia around Barmouth where my father had commanded an Officer Cadet Training Unit at the end of the war, and I loved it. And I had done some travelling to resorts during my tourism survey. But I did not know the industrial heart of South Wales or the rural area of mid Wales. It was a terrific opportunity and I got deep into studying the history of coal mining and steel making and the current problems of unemployment now that these were on the wane. Early in the year I had become a friend of Simon Jenkins, then working as a journalist and columnist on the *Evening Standard*. We had met at the retirement party of Des Wilson, the dynamic founder of the homeless charity Shelter, who had become a friend of mine. When I mentioned to Simon that I was doing a Wales survey he said I must not even begin without meeting his father.

My lunch at the corner table at Bianchi's in Frith Street with the Rev. Daniel Jenkins was memorable. He was a compact, gentle, smiling Welshman, born in the valleys near Merthyr Tydfil and raised a Welsh Congregationalist. A brilliant child, he had won scholarships to Merthyr Grammar, Edinburgh and then Oxford and become an academic theologian, spending 12 years as a professor of theology at Chicago University, serving simultaneously as a congregational minister in England. When I met him he was based at Sussex University and he later went on to be Professor of Theology at Princeton.

So by any standards I was in distinguished company. But to meet this modest person you would not know it. The first thing he asked me was what I knew about rugby. This was very little, though my father had played for Caius College, Cambridge. Rugby was the religion of Wales, Daniel told me, and without knowledge of it I would not begin to understand the culture I was embracing. He recommended that I lunch with Barry John, the dazzling fly half of the Welsh team who had scored brilliantly in the recent Five Nations and, along with Gareth Edwards, was the current star of Welsh rugby. We talked for hours about the Welsh love of opera, male voice choirs, community life in the valleys where he had been brought up and the beauty of the west-coast countryside where he had bought a family house. By the end of our lunch he had completely got me into the mood to embark on my survey. I did indeed give lunch to Barry John – the week he announced that, aged 27, he was going to retire from professional rugby – and my survey, 'Out of the Valleys', opened with a photograph of him converting a try.

I planned my visits to Wales that spring to coincide with the Cardiff season of the Welsh National Opera, settling in the Park Hotel around the corner from the Opera House. That season they were playing Verdi's *Falstaff*, a production that had been premiered two years before to mark the investiture of Prince Charles as Prince of Wales and had starred the Welsh hero baritone Geraint Evans. This season they had lured the great Italian Tito Gobbi to the role. I had seen him in many roles at Covent Garden and was excited by the prospect. In the interval I was standing alone at the bar beside two Welshmen. 'Well, what do you make of him?' said one. 'He's not bad,' said the other, 'but he's not a touch on Geraint.'

At a party given by Hugh Stevenson, editor of the *Times Business News*, I met Ronald Higgins who had been a diplomat with Hugh and now was working on the *Observer*. He had bought a house on the Welsh borders in the Golden Valley in Herefordshire. He had recently divorced from his wife, the journalist Mary Holland, and was, it emerged, something of a walking-wounded man. He invited me to stay in his cottage between a fortnight I was spending in Cardiff. I went. It poured with rain and I got horrible stomach problems eating a duck egg. So it was not a romantic weekend. But he cared for me sweetly and I remember thinking what an interesting and thoughtful man he was and just the man for my sister Libby. About six years later they did get together and were extremely happily married.

While on the *Economist* I also got involved with Women in Media, a women's lib organisation which included Joan Shenton (Simon Jenkins' then girlfriend who worked in TV), Mary Holland, Mary Stott (editor of the *Guardian*'s women's pages), Jill Tweedie of the *Guardian* and many others. Margaret Cruickshank from the American Survey was also a member, but I remember that it was difficult to encourage other women on the *Economist* to join. The likes of Sarah Hogg had made it in a man's world and were not that concerned about the sisterhood. I don't remember the date of the great first women's lib march in 1971 but I do remember that it started at Speakers' Corner at Marble Arch. We marched along Oxford Street, down Regent Street and on to congregate in Trafalgar Square. I was near the front with Margaret and my banner. Passing Liberty in Regent Street I noticed *just* the fabric I fancied on display. Multi-tasking, I bounded inside, bought four yards of beige weave and continued the march waving my bag with its Liberty sign to join the rousing speeches in Trafalgar Square.

Back at the *Economist* I was deep into writing in my Welsh survey about new industries coming into the valleys when the phone rang. 'My name is Graham Watson from Curtis Brown,' the man announced. 'Ah, yes. What is it you make?' I replied. Graham was often to tease me about that. He explained that Curtis Brown was a literary agency of which he was the managing director. They were scouting for a new agent and my friend Virginia Makins from the *Times Educational Supplement* had recommended me as a likely candidate. We arranged to meet for a drink at the Ritz. In the gap between the conversation and our meeting I phoned up Joe Rogaly – I knew he had an agent called Deborah Rogers, who he would phone from Washington and he always insisted that I leave the room when he did that. He made her role sound romantic and mysterious. I phoned him: 'Joe, you know me well. Do you think I would make a good literary agent?' I asked. 'Of course you would,' he replied. 'You adore match-making.'

I met the writer Andrew Sinclair for a drink in El Vino's in Fleet Street. He knew that world and he knew me and loved giving advice. Curtis Brown, he said, was the largest literary agency and prestigious but was in need of livening up – the younger, often female, agents like Deborah Rogers, Diana Crawfurd and Pat Kavanagh were sweeping up the brighter young writers. So it would be a great opportunity to learn. He looked at me in his very serious way and advised: 'One thing. Never sleep with your authors ...' Thus advised, I went off to my life-changing drink at the Ritz.

Graham Watson was a tall, distinguished-looking man with a little beard. He rose to greet me at the Ritz bar. I was wearing a red linen jacket with a green and navy scarf and, I hoped, looked lively enough for this new profession I was contemplating. He suggested we drink champagne.

We immediately hit it off. He wanted to hear about my work and my family – he was exactly my father's age and his own daughters were of a similar age to me. And I wanted to hear what he had in mind for me. Someone had just retired from Curtis Brown so there was a job vacancy. But more importantly they wanted a younger agent who would bring in a new generation of writers to the agency. I said that the idea of a career change was exciting. I knew so little of his world, but it did overlap with mine a lot and I certainly knew a lot of authors.

The next move was to meet his colleagues: the redoubtable Juliet O'Hea, who represented Doris Lessing, Mary Renault, Patrick White and other luminaries; the lively Australian Peter Grose, who was in line to succeed Graham, and eccentric Andrew Best, who was in charge of the more academic list and whose heart was in choral singing. I loved the atmosphere and the idea of a world of books. I took the job to start in September and headed off for a month in India – I hoped that I would be in this job for a long time, so a break was due.

9.

Family Life

Meanwhile, up in Yorkshire since my mother's death my father had been pursued by many ladies. He was a real catch: the local MP in his fifties, an enchanting, good-looking, distinguished man and witty to boot. Libby and Bunny and I became very aware of the ladies as they tried to woo us too. I remember being very struck by one of them, who was an elegant divorcee who showered him with gifts – I still have the monogrammed bath towels. I realised that she had never had a role in life other than as a wife and mother. She had no career to fall back on and I felt really sorry for her in her desperation.

Then one day in summer 1970, Pa sent me a postcard. 'Can you come to Yorkshire this weekend? I have a pretty widow and her son coming to stay.' This turned out to be Cynthia Duncan, a widow of around 50, and her son Alex. I can still picture them sitting in the big bay window area of the sitting room looking at the view across to the Yorkshire Wolds. It became clear to me right away that Cynthia was a serious candidate to be my step-mother. I also got on extremely well with her 20-year-old boy Alex, who was then an undergraduate at Oxford. I rather fancied the idea of a kid brother.

I found Cynthia's background fascinating. She was English but had been married to a South African called Patrick Duncan who was the son of the South African Governor General. But, having worked in the Colonial Service in Lesotho, he had gone into radical South African politics, first in the Liberal Party and later with the Pan Africanist Congress (PAC). They had lived in the Orange Free State just across the border from Lesotho's capital Maseru but had then moved to Cape Town where he ran a magazine called *Contact*.

When he was banned he had escaped his banning order and lived in the mountains in southern Lesotho where she had joined him. He had then made a journey to the UK but had not been allowed back to Lesotho by the British government. The family had ended up in Algeria, where Patrick was first the PAC representative and then worked for an American relief operation. It was in Algeria that he contracted aplastic anaemia from which he died aged 48. Through all this, Cynthia had stood by him and organised her four children. I could see she was a woman with a lot of spunk. Because of my friendship with Joe Rogaly, I was particularly interested in South Africa and knew quite a number of South Africans and the name Patrick Duncan very much resonated with them.

Bunny was living in Cameroon in West Africa doing two years of International Voluntary Service at the time. But Libby and I were introduced later in the year to Cynthia' daughters – 15-year-old Annie and 11-year-old Emma. Her oldest son, Patrick, was living in Tanzania as a zoologist with his young wife, Clare. We also met her brother Jim and his enchanting Yorkshire wife, Anne, who lived in great style in the manor at Hexton in Hertfordshire. Pa already knew Anne's family, the Yorkes, and so that was a happy link. By the end of 1970 Pa and Cynthia were engaged and they got married in May 1971.

Of course, Libby and I wanted Papa to be happy and we liked Cynthia's children we had met a great deal. But it did involve considerable upheaval at Park Farm. For the eight years that my mother had been ill my grandmother Mardy had valiantly looked after much of the domestic life at Park Farm. When married, she had run a large house in Sowerby Bridge with staff and so it came naturally to her. But of course this did not fit in with Cynthia's plans at all. Someone once told me (though apparently it's not true) that the Chinese character for discord is a house with two women in it. Mardy had her own sitting room at the end of the house below her bedroom but was used to being part of the family.

I can't remember the order of things. But Cynthia was very rude to Mardy and I remember once when she and Pa were going out to dinner Mardy was standing in the hall and said, 'Have a good time, Cynthia.' Cynthia slammed the door in her face. I can still see Mardy standing there with her arms out as if paralysed. She turned to me and said, 'What shall I do, darling? You see, I've nowhere to go.' I hugged her and said she must not worry and Libby and I would see she was all right. She was 85, which is a difficult time to move. The next morning I had my first row with Cynthia.

At this time Libby was working as a paediatrician in York Hospital. She had done some of her training in Scarborough and was much respected in the area. She had bought a charming small house in Fulford, a village which had become a suburb of York and was close to Heslington, home of the newish York University. So Libby had a good independent life with lots of friends, many of whom taught or worked at the university. The last thing she needed was her grandmother in her spare room. But it became more and more clear that Mardy could not stay at Park Farm. It was agony for Pa because he had relied on Mardy looking after my mother for so long and felt very guilty but helpless.

So Mardy started spending weekends with Libby and with great luck a ground-floor flat was found next door into which Mardy moved. While the circumstances were sad, there is no doubt that the change was a perfect solution. At 85 Mardy rose to the occasion, made many brand-new friends in the village, including a charming widow who lived across the road and who she saw every day. Our family friend Rosemary Preston would bring her young daughter to tea every Tuesday with her friends after school and Mardy would hold a bingo party. My godmother Dorothy Davidson would visit regularly and reported that Mardy had become part of Fulford life.

It also worked better for me. I would drive up from London on Friday evening, spend the night with Lib and see Mardy and then sometimes go over to Park Farm the next day. At about this time Bunny returned from North Cameroon. She did not feel welcome at Park Farm and her room had been redecorated as a spare room in her absence. She was planning to do a teacher training course and, as she had lost her base, did it in York and stayed with Libby for a year.

This was not a happy time for Bunny. She had loved her time in North Cameroon and made good friends there. Her boyfriend – whose name escapes me – visited her there and they travelled together. But clearly this was not a success. It was during her travels in Upper Volta (later Burkina Faso) that Bunny had a revelation. She described it to me later. She was on a bus in the countryside and God called her. She knew that she had a calling to serve him. But back in England she could not see a way to do this. She became very depressed.

After her year of training she got a job teaching in Woodstock near Oxford. She lived in a flat in North Oxford across the gardens from Deborah Cowen, the sister of Cynthia's former husband Patrick Duncan, and her daughters Di and Gina. Deb had been married in South Africa, had her two daughters, but had parted from her law professor husband when they were living in Chicago and she decided to settle in Oxford where she had been an undergraduate. She was a wonderful encourager to Bunny, as she was to many young people. She also had the problem that Cynthia would not speak to her – for some unknown historic reason – and so she could understand Bunny's upset.

It was while she was there that she became involved with the church of St Ebbes, which led her later to train for the priesthood. One evening when Bunny was living in Oxford I invited her to Covent Garden along with friends. Our fourth member of the party dropped out and so I invited Ronald Higgins at the last minute. He and Bunny took one look at each other and began a relationship which lasted well over a year. At that time Ronald was working at the *Observer* but used to weekend in Herefordshire. He would pick Bunny up from Oxford on his way.

Bunny was still struggling with her calling at that point. And she later parted from Ronald and became involved with a very unsatisfactory man who she met through her church. He was part of some religious organisation in South Africa and Bunny visited him there. The bonus of that trip was that she met and got to know Alex's aunt and uncle, John and Pam Duncan, in Plettenberg Bay, who simply adored her. Finally, Bunny did take the plunge and went to train for the priesthood – even though she would not be allowed to practise it – at St John's College, Nottingham, where she was extremely happy.

Meanwhile, Mardy flourished in Fulford for ten years – I have photos of her delightful ninetieth-birthday lunch. Then the inevitable fall meant she had to live her last five years in a home in York. But it was a lovely home and she was adored there. In 1987 she had her hundredth birthday surrounded by great-grandchildren. I have a picture of her with my Alice and Max – aged six and four – and Bunny's first child, Elizabeth. On her lap is our ten-week-old, Ben. They were a hundred years apart.

One memory of Mardy I treasure. In the late 70s I was staying next door with Libby and came into Mardy's bedroom with her early-morning cup of tea. There she sat looking so pretty in her lacy jacket. I asked how she had slept. 'One of the things they don't tell you about growing old', she said, 'is that quite often when you wake up in the morning you think you are dead!' 'Goodness! What does it feel like?' I asked. 'Well, you lie there feeling wonderfully peaceful. Then, very slowly, all your aches and pains begin and you realise that you are not dead at all! And you think: "Oh bother!"'

10.

Larry and Travels 1970–73

In my messy, bulging files there is a particularly messy, bulging one called 'Letters' into which I dropped every letter I wanted to keep. At some point I must have sorted them a bit and there is a separate file among the letters called 'Larry'. There are 37 letters ranging from crinkly, almost illegible ones from Saigon to Phnom Penh to Bangkok, later Cuba and Mexico. And there are lots from Washington. When he dated his letters he rarely wrote the year. So it gets confusing. They are warm, funny, gossipy letters full of cryptic information and wise observation. There is a lot about our mutual friends – Walter and Ann, the Justs, Peter Osnos, John and Elizabeth Midgley, Sally Quinn and Ben Bradlee – and also a lot about his concerns about his children. Above all there are regular declarations of love for me.

Larry had not been a letter writer and so was surprised when, back in England, I started bombarding him with my news. But once he got into the habit he was a magical correspondent.

When, to the bewilderment of all, Larry died in August 1979, aged 50, I rushed to Washington for his funeral. I had been staying with him only in June for his fiftieth birthday party. He was so alive to me. When I returned home I went back to those letters. I remember reading them, deeply upset. And I remember thinking, 'I blew it.' Here was a man who had loved – indeed adored – me unreservedly and I had thrown it away. I had not felt ready to commit and then had married someone else whose love was not that reliable and it had ended in sadness. I would never find love like that again. As it turned out, I did. And when it happened I recognised it and did not let Alex go.

Forty years on I am looking at those letters again. I had forgotten how long we continued to see each other. In May 1972 he wrote:

> *Once again: 1) Not the faintest change in the unreserved way I've loved you the past three years, 2) It would be emotional death for me to have anything less from you (realising this sort of thing may have gone out of fashion.) 3) If you can ever sort out your fears and ambivalence and really let yourself go, I would spray and powder and eschew shiny suits and do all things but wear a ring through my nose ...*

That first summer of 1970 in London, Larry's daughter Cathy Stern came to stay with me for the month of August and I took her on trips to Yorkshire where I have pictures of her with my grandmother Mardy, who she loved. Then we went on a magic visit to the Welsh borders with

Lucilla. Later Larry joined us and he and I went to Ireland for a week, seeing Dublin and then driving across the country to Cork. It was our first visit to Ireland and we loved it. I remember standing by a wild lake and a huge swan flying low and close and Larry saying, 'Leda just didn't get out of the way.' We then went for a weekend in Paris and had such a happy time there that I stole the bathmat at the Hotel Belles Feuilles as a souvenir. In late autumn he was back and we had a marvellous weekend in the Cotswolds of which I have photos of me in the Broadway Hotel.

In autumn 1971, he went to Washington where the *Post* persuaded him to return from Saigon and take over the running of their new Style section. In my diary I see that Larry visited me on 30 December 1971 and then saw me off to Africa on 1 January. It was during that visit that I said I could not imagine us not being together and that I agreed that I would return to Washington to be with him. I can even remember when I was in Uganda looking at brightly coloured cotton kangas and thinking I would decorate a room in our Washington home with them.

In late March 1972, we were in Paris – my diary shows dinner at Le Procope. Cathy had made me aware that there was a woman in Washington called Turri who was pursuing him. She was divorced and had teenage children like Larry so it was an obvious fit. However, Cathy was not keen on the idea. I remember Larry wearing a very posh dressing gown, which he would never have bought for himself, which I guessed had been a gift from this lady. We even talked about her in Paris. I can't remember the order of things. But by the end of our visit, having said I wanted to be with him, I could not quite go through with it.

I returned to England and he wrote that Turri was pressuring him to marry. Then one day I got a telegram that said, 'Marriage balloon goes up Sunday.' That would be 16 April. I was distressed and shocked. But I knew I had only myself to blame. That weekend of Larry's marriage I by coincidence had Izzy and Esther Stone coming to dinner. They were on their annual European trip, which involved crossing on an ocean liner (because they loved to dance) and visiting Venice and London. I had arranged a gathering – including Anthony Harris from the FT and Bud Nossiter, the *Washington Post* correspondent – of people who would enjoy Izzy and I can see him now in my front room holding forth to this selected group of my friends.

I was getting the supper ready in the kitchen and Esther came to talk. She asked after Larry. I said that actually he was getting married to Turri the next day. Whereupon Esther gave out a shriek: 'Do you hear that, Izzy? Larry is getting married to that dreadful Turri woman.' Izzy was visibly shocked and for the whole meal they both seemed distracted, with Esther muttering periodically, 'I just can't believe this.' So the dinner could not have been called a success.

The postscript to this was that years later, when I had just parted from my husband, Alasdair – of whom Izzy and Esther approved – he and I decided to come back together for the evening to give a lively dinner at Alasdair's flat as if we were still together. Izzy and Esther longed for me to be happy and I could just not face their distress at another failed romance. The dinner – with included John Julius Norwich because of the Venice connection – went off brilliantly. Mary Hughes – who was by now Mary Venturini, having married Franco, a dashing Italian journalist – was present. She said afterwards that it was the oddest event she had been to and she could not understand how I carried it off.

Sally Quinn gave me a vivid and unflattering picture of the wedding, which was of a very alternative sort with Larry looking very uncomfortable. It was a failure. By late November Larry had moved out. On 28 November he wrote:

> What happened, you ask. In a nutshell it was a question of marrying someone you weren't in love with while at the same time loving someone else. And so despite undying attentions, patient vigils, ever-burning fire in fireplace, Nantucket summer house, trust funds, nice children, tender attentions to my own drifting waifs, I had to pull myself out like an abscessed tooth ... Three magic carpet rides on the shrink couch of Dr Herbert Cohen. For Turri's sake, he told me, 'I want you out.'
>
> There was too much possessiveness, too many shaggy young persons coming, going milling with their wet amorphous minds: too much goodness, broken wings coming for mending with toys, alcohol (for the middle aged). Too much overfuckingpowering solicitude. And so night after night I ended up grinding my teeth, scarring the palms and thumb balls with my nails, old duodenal pain trilling high C over high C, staring up and hating myself for the whole hideous mess being allowed to happen in the illusory pursuit of worthiness, sensibleness.

How could one resist a letter like that? Of course, Larry and I would remain close for years to come.

Africa

In January 1972 I visited Africa for the first time and it really blew me away. I have been fascinated ever since. My visit was triggered first by Laurie Cockcroft, who was working for the Tanzanian government in Dar es Salaam; then by Dick and Barbara Slater, who were by now ensconced in the High Commission in Uganda; and finally, by the wish to meet my step-brother Patrick in the Serengeti in Northern Tanzania. So I plotted my three-week journey.

Staying with Laurie was a wonderful introduction. His knowledge of Africa was great and I was intrigued by Tanzania, led by its idealistic but clearly impractical socialist president Julius Nyerere. I read up all about Ujamaa villages where the inhabitants would live communally but which were not proving a success. Tanzania was very poor. It was clear that Laurie was very at home there. His friends were an interesting mix of Tanzanians and European aid types, all of whom I found intriguing to talk to. We visited Bagamoyo and I explored Dar when Laurie was working.

While there I visited Zanzibar, which, at that point while technically part of Tanzania, was very separate from the mainland. I spent a day at the port in Dar trying to fix to go on a traditional dhow. But this proved impossible. I ended up on a put-put plane, which landed me in Zanzibar in one piece. I settled myself in the charming Zanzibar Hotel in Stone Town – the only hotel on the island – with its exquisite carved doorways and chests. On arrival I sat in the dining room having my coffee and fell into conversation with a large Tanzanian who seemed to be the only other guest. He turned out to be Wilbert Chagula, who was the Minister for Water Development from the mainland and of course a friend of

Laurie's. He was glad I had travelled well: 'When I took that flight the emergency exit fell into the sea.'

I remember conversations with him about the government of this new country – Tanzania gained independence in 1961. We talked about the railway that the Chinese were building into the interior. He liked dealing with the Chinese, he said. They understood Africa better than the USSR. 'You know something? The Russians sent Ghana a snow plough!'

Also at the hotel I met some American marine biologists who were working in Zanzibar. They drove me over to the other side of this long, narrow island to see the beaches that faced the Indian Ocean. I was stunned, for they were as beautiful as anything I had seen in the Caribbean and were completely empty. If things change for this country, I thought, then this could be the most stunning holiday resort. As it turned out, when Zanzibar did finally open up for tourism, they learned the lesson of Kenya – which had gone for the cheap package market in the 60s and 70s with ugly high-rise hotels – and aimed at a more discerning tourist. The rule was that no hotel could be taller than a palm tree and the result when we visited as a family in 2000 was enchanting.

After a week in Dar, I headed off north by bus to Moshi where I would change buses and head west for the Serengeti. I loved my bus trip. The company was positively boisterous. Everyone was so very welcoming. I remember my neighbour quizzing me about my age. He could not believe that I was as much as 26, was not married and looked so young. I produced my passport as evidence and he asked all our neighbours to guess my age – rather like guess the weight of the cake.

From Moshi, where I stayed at a YMCA, I headed to Arusha and my new bus drove on towards Seronera where Patrick lived. Darkness falls fast in Africa and in the gloaming the bus stopped at Ngorongoro Crater and everyone started getting out. It turned out we were not going to Seronera that night. I asked the driver where I could stay. There was a lodge five miles back, he said. 'Don't worry,' said my neighbour Joachim – a young Kikuyu who I had been chatting with – 'You can stay with me.' I must have looked cautious. 'Don't worry,' he said, 'I have many sisters. You can sleep with them.'

He lifted my suitcase onto his head and off we headed down the crater in the darkness. His home turned out to be a wooden hut, which doubled as the local village shop run by his mother, with two thatched rondavels for sleeping. I was introduced to all the family, shown the bed I would share with his sister Monica and then settled down to hot, sweet tea with his father. He had two families, he told me – one outside the park and this one in – and drove one of the zebra-striped minibuses for tourists in the crater.

I ate supper of mealie meal and gravy alone with the father, served by his wife and daughters who were eating next door. Then everyone came in to drink more hot, sweet tea. I felt quite extraordinarily privileged to be, by happy mistake, having this very African experience. I said how grateful I was and then remembered that on leaving Gatwick Airport I had grabbed a few presents in case they came in handy. I shall always treasure the scene squatting around the fire when my surprised hosts took the After Eight chocolates out of their little individual parcels, admiring the packaging in awe. 'Yum, yum!' said Pa. 'Very good for safari!'

Next morning, neighbours dropped by to meet this surprise guest and I was introduced to some local Maasai who came shopping. Finally, I was sent on my way with a friend of theirs who was driving a beer truck to Seronera. He delivered me with panache to the front door of my new step-brother Patrick's house at Seronera. There he was with his wife, Clare, and my other step-brother Alex.

My following days were a major treat. Patrick was a truly striking young man aged 24. All his life he had been passionate about nature and animals in general and had read Zoology at Oxford. Now he was at the Serengeti Research Institute working on material for his PhD thesis on a large antelope called a topi. His enthusiasm for the Serengeti wildlife and for his specific work was entirely infectious. We went on amazing drives, sighting lions, rhino and all manner of birds and beasts. I remember one evening picking up an ostrich egg that was so heavy the contents made us nine strong-tasting omelettes.

Clare seemed a very gentle person but clearly someone of great resolve. She had known Patrick before they met at Oxford as her father, Morrice James, had been a close friend of Patrick's father, also called Patrick. To complicate matters, Morrice, a widower with two daughters and a son, had become officially engaged to Cynthia soon after she was widowed by her husband, Patrick. But once the wedding plans were afoot Morrice had backed out – to Cynthia's obvious distress. So when their children became close as Oxford undergraduates and then announced that they wanted to marry, it was a shock to both Morrice and Cynthia. What's more they wanted to marry soon, as Patrick was heading off to Africa. Morrice did not attend the wedding and Clare left Oxford without finishing her degree. Now Clare was very much in wifely mode – baking the daily bread and involving herself as much as possible in Patrick's work. But it was a pretty isolating situation for a young and clever woman.

The reason that Alex was there was that his life had been greatly disrupted the previous summer. He had graduated from Oxford and had been set to head off to a teaching job in Botswana. But he had been involved in a head-on car accident while living at Hexton in Hertfordshire. The man in the other car who had caused the crash had died instantly. Alex had been left with a broken jaw and a broken thigh bone and his Botswana plans had to be dropped. He was still in recovery mode.

After five days of glorying in the beauty of the wide Serengeti plains, the vast skies of Africa and loving getting to know my new step-brother Patrick and enjoying the company of Alex, I headed off on a bus to Musoma on Lake Victoria where I would catch a steamer. These ferries sailed clockwise around the lake and were run by East African Railways and carried rail carriages as well as goods and people. I spent two nights on a ferry and loved the trip. I travelled second class and it was extremely sociable. We stopped off at the colourful port of Mwanza, which seemed like one huge market and where the trains were put on tracks to take them to Dar es Salaam. Finally, after a 19-hour journey, I arrived with the dawn at Port Bell Entebbe in Uganda to be met by Dick Slater's secretary.

At breakfast in the High Commission residence, Dick was apologetic about not coming to greet me. Today was the monthly meeting that President Idi Amin held with the heads of foreign missions. These meetings could be very erratic. Anything could happen. Indeed, last month the president had suggested a scheme to form his Cabinet into a football team to play the heads of foreign missions. Everyone was sincerely hoping that he had forgotten this plan.

By lunch Dick was more relaxed. Amin had been in warm form and the football scheme had not been brought up. The way that Dick and other Brits I met discussed Amin was interesting. It was as if they were talking about a not very bright but perfectly benevolent child. Idi Amin had been in power for a year, having ousted Milton Obote in an army coup. Dick had found Obote impossibly difficult to deal with when he and Barbara arrived in 1970 and so had not been upset when the coup happened. In fact, he was probably responsible for the fact that Britain was the first country to recognise Amin's regime.

I remember that one day several senior British army officers came to lunch. They were part of a team training the Ugandan army. The man beside me clearly knew Amin well. I asked about him. 'I was his commander,' he said. 'I trained him in the British Army. Not much up there' – pointing to his head – 'but a good sort.' Of course he turned out to be a tyrant and when in August that year he evicted Uganda's East African Asian population – around 35,000 people, many of whom came to Britain – he evicted Dick and Barbara too, doing so on public television. It was Dick's last posting.

I did not see much outside Kampala on my three days there. But I loved the city and the lush and hilly landscape. I found the Ugandans that I met both warm and engaging and I loved spending time with Barbara. By my bedside was a copy of *Drum* by Anthony Sampson, who I knew from Washington. It told the story of his going out to South Africa as a young journalist and being employed by Jim Bailey to run a magazine for a black audience. I was gripped by his description of South Africa in the 50s and 60s as it involved the Duncan family, who were great friends of the Baileys. And indeed their aunt Deborah had worked on *Drum*.

My next stop was Nairobi from where I would fly to London. I was really keen to travel by day to see the countryside. The smart, fast buses went by night. So I ended up on a crowded rickety bus with chickens aboard as we drove through the thrilling mountainous countryside. I shall never forget the last bit of the journey as we drove through the old Kenyan White Highlands and I saw the sun set on the Rift Valley. No wonder the British wanted to settle here. It had much in common with England with its rolling hills and greenery – but a much better climate.

India

Back in London life went on but by July 1972 I had given my notice at the *Economist*. I hoped I would be in my new job at Curtis Brown for a long time, so I decided to take a proper break in India with the Lankesters in Delhi as my base. In mid-August I flew 14 hours to Delhi, reading Ruth Prawer Jhabvala's *An Experience of India* to get me in the mood. Tim and Tricia by now had two children – Alex had been born in April 1970 and Olivia in late 1971 – and had moved into a charming house complete with live-in servants. In my diary I write: 'Alexandra is now delightful and very composed indeed. The tantrums of England have gone – which only goes to show how children need a regular life.'

On arrival I found there was another guest in the form of Christopher Beauman. I had known of Chris and his wife Sally in Washington, where they had lived, but they left for London just before I got there. They had been good friends of John Graham and other journalists. They had then moved back to London because Sally had got a brilliant job as editor of *Queen* magazine. Chris had gone into banking. Tim always said that Chris should have been a civil servant. He had the right intellect for it. But Sally had wanted him to earn proper money. Whether this was the case I don't know. But sadly the marriage had collapsed anyway when she had fallen for Alan Howard, the actor who was being famously successful at the Royal Shakespeare Company and who she had interviewed when he was playing a jaw-stopping Hamlet.

So Chris was touring India nursing a broken heart. I was not exactly nursing a broken heart, but I had been pretty upset when another man with whom I was having a budding relationship had upped and married his old girlfriend while I was on a holiday with my American friends Ward and Ann Just in Brittany in July. I had returned to a letter on the mat telling me this.

My plan had been to settle in with the Lankesters, get my bearings and arrange various trips. But Chris, who was extraordinarily well organised, was leaving on a tour of Rajasthan the next day. Everything was fixed so why did I not come with him? Tricia and Tim encouraged me. And so off we set the next morning by bus to Jaipur. It was my first sight of proper Indian countryside as I watched it pass by for six or so hours on a crowded bus on an often bumpy road. In my diary I wrote: 'The evening sunlight bathed the land which was verdant and watery as can be after the monsoon. The sun set behind the hills and then the nearly full moon took over giving quite marvellous reflections in the water and creating incredible shadow around the Jaipur hills. We saw camels for the first time. As we came over the hill to Jaipur the whole of the valley was full of moonlight and the domes of the Maharaja's brother's palace were illuminated.'

Jaipur was stunning with its extraordinary pink palaces and vibrant street life, not to mention magical craftwork. We stayed in a simple but clean hotel. I wrote: 'The bustle, noise and chaos of an Indian street is the stuff of excitement: camels collide with rickshaws, colliding with bullock carts while eccentrically painted buses incessantly hoot a path through the melee.' We visited Amber, the old palace in the hills outside the town with its spectacular views and extraordinary rooms with sparkling mirror-work. My diary has a watercolour of the view from Amber with the lush hills each topped with a little temple or folly on top. Then we were off to Udaipur by overnight train, leaving at 6.30 p.m. and arriving at 9.00 a.m.

A feature of travelling in India is long train journeys – and I loved them. We chose first class, which was comfortable, wonderfully old-fashioned and remarkably cheap for us Europeans. Trains were also an intriguing opportunity to talk to Indians – those who travelled by train not being the grandees (who flew) but professional classes who generally spoke good English. I found this particularly later when I was travelling on my own. My diary tells of Chris on the Udaipur train having an absorbing conversation with 'an ebullient man from the Reserve Bank in Bombay who spent most of his time fixing village agricultural credit and regaled us for hours about peasants not accepting advice, politicians swiping the money etc. etc. For all this he was a great optimist: "The past 10 years seem for everyone to have been the period where modern ideas have begun to latch on."'

In Udaipur we stayed two nights with Bal Malik. He was a prosperous Sikh from Delhi who had very radical politics. He was living as a teacher and was a friend of Tim and Tricia. But I was also keen to meet him as he was married to my school friend Diana Maclehose, who had met him when she was working with Tibetan refugees and who I had seen with Tricia in Delhi. They had one child but were now living apart and Bal was involved with a radical feminist called Kamla Bhasin. They were altogether extremely stimulating and informative about Indian politics and the politics of Rajasthan. I wrote: 'Bal used to teach at the Doon School (a large British-style public school north of Delhi) and then went south to Kerala to start his own school. He has only been in Udaipur for two years. He must have been an exciting man to live with and exhausting and aggravating to be actually married to.'

We visited Udaipur's famous lake palaces and were generally bowled over. Then more journeys, first via Ranakpur – which included some broken-down buses – to Jodhpur with its stunning palace above the town and then an overnight train again to Jaisalmer way out north in the desert near the Pakistan border. In all this Chris was a great companion. We also shared books. Chris was an annoyingly fast reader and managed to absorb the content at such speed that I was really envious. I remember us both reading Ford Madox Ford's *The Good Soldier* and discussing it intently together.

In Jaisalmer we were captivated by the intricately carved sandstone Jain temples and the extraordinary sophisticated carving on the domestic houses. It had always been an important trading point and clearly a place of great wealth. Then overnight to Jodhpur where I was so tired that I went to sleep after lunch in the tourist bungalow and 'had a lovely dream about Larry and as a result woke with the heaviest heart imaginable and was forced to walk in the Lady Willingdon Gardens for hours thinking of lost opportunities which I would still not take if offered again'. The stuff of depression, but not, it appeared, more than a good meal at the Talk of the Town could cure ...

All these journeys were very long and when we got overnight to Bikener I felt very tired and suggested to Chris that we skip it and get a train to Delhi. He was shocked and adamant that we should stick to his schedule. It was worth it of course. So it was that we arrived, nine days after our departure, exhausted in Delhi. But it had been a spellbinding and informative trip and in Chris I had made a really good friend.

After a couple of days recuperating, I flew to Calcutta where I stayed with Padma, the sister-in-law of Tricia's Delhi friend Bim, in great elegance in a large nineteenth-century colonial white house. Somehow it was the wealth of Calcutta that took me by surprise. I wrote: 'I am having my first taste of Indian wealthy business community life.' Padma taught at the American School as well as running a shop selling saris that she had printed herself. I considered her liberated but 'she says this is not so and has a good line in stories about her male chauvinist husband. She did, however, come out with the bold remark that by 60 she hoped to take a lover.'

Padma took me with some friends to tea at the historic Tollygunge Club, a country club founded in 1895 for polo-playing Brits but now frequented by elegant Indians with its tennis, golf, etc. It was amazingly posh. But on the journey out through the south of Calcutta I saw incredible poverty, which my hosts were obviously entirely accustomed to. Calcutta colonial architecture in general quite blew me away.

Next day, I flew to Dhaka in Bangladesh – flying was the only option as all the rail bridges had been destroyed in the war the year before. I had been keen to go because of my connection with Fazle Hasan Abed and his friends in London working for Action Bangladesh. Since then Marietta, his girlfriend who had come out to visit him in Bangladesh, had returned to England and committed suicide. On arrival I went to see him. I wrote: 'Abed has given up Shell and is now running an aid programme in Sylhet – the area in the north where his family had tea gardens ... Sitting at his desk in his pink shirt, Abed looked like an extremely wise 23-year-old. But he is in fact 33. His relief programme is designed as a concentrated model of what could happen in other parts of Bangladesh if the government felt like it.' I went on: 'It is staggeringly disheartening to find so soon after independence that all the policemen are lining their pockets just as quickly as they can at the expense of the people. That, I fear, is what finished Marietta.'

That evening I had supper with Abed. His programme was called BRAC – the Bangladesh Rural & Advancement Committee. I was not to see Abed again for many decades. Over 30 years he built BRAC from a small organisation working with refugee families after the civil war into the largest NGO in the world, working in health, micro-finance, agriculture and education, not just in Bangladesh but also in other poor countries in post-conflict situations like Afghanistan and South Sudan.

Abed had arranged for me to stay with his brother Juned and his wife, Nafisa, in Dhaka. Juned spoke good English, though Nafisa did not. They had a charming baby called Nabila, and I was made so very welcome. While there I travelled around quite a bit and made friends with Lewis Simons, the *Washington Post* correspondent. I had a deal with Brian Beedham at the *Economist* that I could do some pieces for him there. It was of course a fascinating opportunity. The country was in political turmoil and elections were planned for the following year. The Awami League, which, under Sheikh Mujibur Rahman, had been the independence force behind the civil war, was in the ascendant and I remember attending huge rallies in the rain with Lewis. I also visited tragic refugee camps nearby and also camps for people who had worked for the previous administration and were now fearful of what would happen to them. I remember being so surprised by how beautiful Bangladesh was. The watery light and the preponderance of all manner of boats made me think of an eastern version of Holland.

On my last evening Juned and Nafisa took me out to a farewell Chinese dinner. I wrote:

Afterwards Juned and I talked about Marietta, who they miss so much. She had stayed with them for six weeks working every day at the Bangladesh Hospital. He said that he thought she eventually chose to leave because her association with Abed's programme put him under suspicion of being in Western (i.e. CIA) hands. They were simply baffled by her suicide. 'We Bengalis do not much commit suicide,' he said, 'I think in the West it is more frequently done.' Like me they felt they had never known her properly, that she was very private. But they said the same about Abed. He has never said anything about Marietta to them. When they asked him when he would be married he would just shrug and smile. 'I don't think now that Abed will be married. He was so long with Marietta. It is difficult to change. But a man must have a wife otherwise he will be very much unhappy when he is old. Abed does not know what country he belongs to. He was 13 years in England. We think he is very English. You must think he is very Bengali. It is a problem for him.'

From Dhaka I returned to Calcutta where I spent the day filing my copy for the *Economist* as Lewis had warned me that if I filed it from Dhaka the censors might stop it. I stayed again with Padma and then headed by train south to Puri, by the sea in Orissa, where I stayed at the Railway Hotel and visited the stunning nearby thirteenth-century temples at Konark. Puri is a major pilgrimage site for Hindus with its famous Jagannath Temple. But the thing I remember most is the wide beach with its thundering waves. In order to swim I had to employ an elderly man wearing a wicker hat who would accompany me into the waves. In Puri I went wild buying fabrics and began to run out of money. So I had to come back second class in the luggage rack reading *Never Kiss a Stranger*, which was the only English-language alternative to *How to Make Friends and Influence People* at Puri Station.

I shall never forget the scene arriving at Calcutta Station. I wrote: 'My heart is by now very hardened. If it were not I would not have had enjoyment in my travels as more and more beggars with stumps as arms and legs, lifeless eyes and weird malformations came shouting "bakshish, bakshish" relentlessly. But Calcutta station made me tremble. Hundreds of seemingly lifeless bodies were huddled up in the enormous entrance area, the lucky ones having found a sack or something to lie on. This is where they sleep. They are homeless.'

Then it was on to Benares and back to Tim and Tricia in Delhi, where I had some perfect days enjoying their Delhi domestic life and having clothes tailored for me. From there, I would return home from India and my literary agent life at Curtis Brown would start.

The following spring I went to Washington again. Larry was divorced and we were still devoted to each other. There were lovely meetings with the Midgleys, Izzy and Esther and the usual suspects. I have a charming picture of Larry and Midgley and me at a lunch party in Midgley's garden. Then Larry and I flew off to Haiti. I can't remember how we got there as it was not an island many tourists visited. But I had been fascinated by the world that Graham Greene had drawn in his novel *The Comedians* and had arranged for us to stay in the Hotel Oloffson, where Greene had hung out, with its enticing wooden 'gingerbread' architecture, which is the French legacy to Haiti. We loved it.

Port-au-Prince was beautiful in many ways and its long-time dictator Papa Doc Duvalier – who had died only two years before – had also built himself some magnificent white buildings. The multi-coloured shacks that spotted the hillsides were vibrant, but poverty was everywhere to be seen and the children's hair was often yellowed – indicating malnutrition. But overall the atmosphere was intoxicating, despite the sinister-looking policemen – Papa Doc's famous Tonton Macoutes – with their dark, dark glasses, who hung around the hotel.

Haiti's infrastructure was very basic. We made a plan to set off across the island to Jacmel, a French colonial town on the southern coast famous for its architecture. To get there we had to rent a four-wheel-drive truck complete with drivers and we shared this with a plucky British family who were there with small children. It took us a whole day to cross the island, the roads being mostly formed of mud, and a lot of getting out and pushing went on. But when we arrived it was worth it. The town was spellbinding.

We stayed in an oh-so-basic hotel where our rooms were divided by canvas walls so everything was public. From this we ventured around town. The colonnaded streets put you in mind of a nineteenth-century French seaside town and were indeed begun by French architects. There was a major art scene there. We visited artists' homes and modest galleries, looking at beguiling sculptures and paintings, and both of us came away with oil paintings of this thrilling and distinctive primitive school. In Jacmel you did not feel that you were in a police state. The people were poor but there was not the feeling of the difference between black and white people that I had felt in much of my Caribbean travels, and I remember thinking: 'Well, it's a mess. But it's their mess.' At some point I discovered that an exquisite white, gingerbread house of good size could be bought for $4,000. Larry, ever impractical and romantic, was tempted to buy.

As it turned out, Haiti did become more popular under the less severe rule of Baby Doc Duvalier. Five years after our visit, in 1978 in Boulder, Colorado, a man came up to me at an event. He asked if I remembered meeting him at the Hotel Oloffson in 1973. I looked blank. Apparently I had been raving about Jacmel and he had gone there, bought a house and its value had rocketed when a proper road had opened, bringing many celebrities to holiday there. He had me to thank for his investment. Many things have happened to Jacmel since, not least that it was hit hard by the 2010 earthquake, which suddenly brought it to the attention of the world and moved Unesco to judge its historic centre a World Heritage Site.

As always, Larry and I had had a perfect and funny holiday together. But it was to be our last. I do remember sneaking a postcard to my new friend Alasdair Clayre from Port-au-Prince and wondering if it would arrive.

Tricia, Tim, Alex and Livy
Lankester, Delhi

From my India diary

With Patrick in the Serengeti

My wedding with Alasdair

With Ben Bradlee and Sally Quinn

John Julius Norwich

Gerry and Lee Durrell

FELICITY !

Agent who fulfills my needs,
I've just received your kindly screeds -
Received by me with joy unbounded -
But now to prove your fears unfounded,
To prove that I am feeling better,
Send you an ILLUSTRATED LETTER!

What to say of La Belle France
Where arteries never have a chance?
Where every menu points with glee
The way to adiposity;
With all that wine and crispy bread...
(One more coronary - I'm dead).

Mushrooms, big as white umbrellas -
They're minus calories they tell us -
But simmered slow in wine and cream:
Dieter's nightmare! Glutton's dream!
But roasted truffles are the best...
(What's that hammering in my chest?).

Shall I speak of hen or duckling,
Quails and pigeons, pigs still suckling?
They say these things make you obese,
Like livers from whole flocks of geese
Moving like huge drifts of snow...
(One more coronary to go).

Oh, how the veg's make you tremble
When in the markets they assemble:
Crisp green lettuce, dark green bean,
Shining eggplant, quite obscene,
Cooked in wine and oil and butter...
(My heart then gave a tiny flutter).

Now the fruits - they're all in season,
Enough to undermine one's reason.
Strawberry, peaches, merry cherry
And grapes, most subtle of the berry -
A berry you can drink and eat...
(Oh, damn, my heart then missed a beat).

Do not think these other dishes
Have dragged my mind away from fishes -
Salmon, rouget, turbot stout
Tie with carp and bream and trout,
While lobster red and ecrevisse...
(A heart attack's a quick release).

To moisten all this provender
Wines that leave you in a blur:
Whites like blondes at St. Tropez,
Reds that sap your will away,
Champagnes into goblets rustle...
(Hear my arteries a-bustle).

Ah! Belle France, you promised land,
Come, we'll walk now, hand in hand
With oyster, snail and bread and butter
And vintages to make you stutter;

Creamy cheese that eats so well
(Or others with atrocious smell);

Hams and salmon, sunset pink,
Fiery Armagnac to drink;

The wrinkled walnut, sugared marron,
Where'er we walk you are not barren:

You fill my glass, you pile my plate,
'Tis you who've got me in this state.

Belle France, I love you, there's no doubt,
But one thing I must just point out -

That here and now I do attest
YOU caused my cardiac arrest!

ENVOI

Felicity, my dearest girl,
Do not cast me as a churl,

But I must end, cast down my quill,
Assuring you I love you still -

So please don't think of me a sinner -
But - seven o'clock -

It's time for dinner.

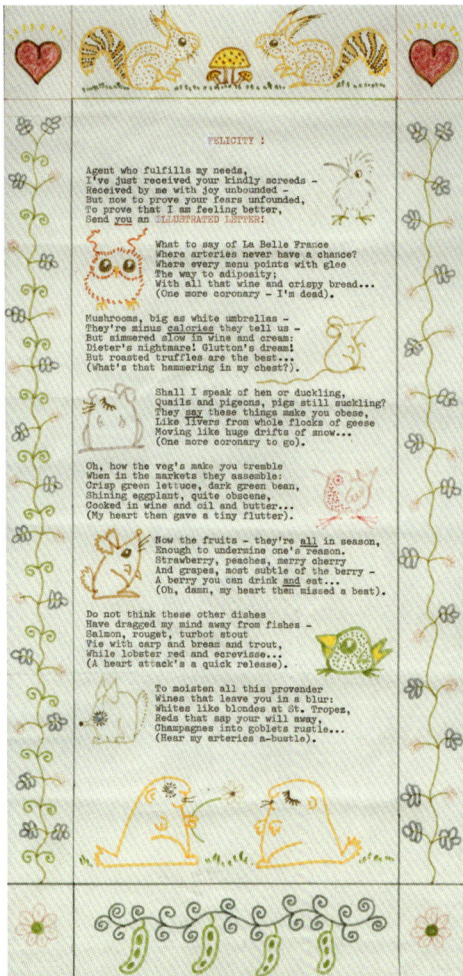

Gerry Durrell's illustrated letter

With Alex in Lesotho

Libby marries Ronald Higgins in 1978 (with many sets of twins)

With Larry at his fiftieth birthday party

With Larry and Midgley

11.

Curtis Brown

———◦———◇———◦———

Looking back at the Curtis Brown I joined in 1972 from today, where huge international corporations dominate publishing, it is amazing to think how small scale it all was then. Curtis Brown had offices in King Street, Covent Garden, the heart of the publishing world. I would describe their offices as shabby chic. Just up the road was Victor Gollancz, run by the founder's fearsome daughter Livia. Walking distance away in Bedford Square were Michael Joseph, Jonathan Cape, Hutchinson, Bodley Head, Secker & Warburg and others occupying charming Georgian buildings. These were all independent publishers of hardback trade books.

Weidenfeld & Nicolson was quaintly south of the river. But that was because it was handy for George Weidenfeld's brilliant apartment on Cheyne Walk where in his time he had lavishly entertained everyone from Golda Meir and Lyndon Johnson to Antonia Fraser. Collins had palatial offices in St James's Street, where Billy Collins ran the show and his dynamic wife ran the successful religious list. John Murray occupied its traditional elegant home in Albemarle Street where Byron, Darwin and Jane Austen had hung out. The mercurial André Deutsch was in Museum Street; Chatto & Windus, round the corner, was run by the terrifying Nora Smallwood. She was godmother to my boss Graham Watson's daughter Julia. It was all very cosy.

Authors also had much cosier relationships with their publishers than they do today. A publisher accepted your first novel and then you walked into the sunset together, hoping and expecting that the editor would become your lifelong editor and friend. And it often happened. Editors did not move jobs much, authors rarely moved publishers and many authors did not have – or feel the need for – literary agents. Old Jock Murray's spare room in Hampstead was often occupied by the likes of Freya Stark, Paddy Leigh Fermor or Dervla Murphy recuperating from their travels.

British publishing in the 70s was almost entirely family businesses publishing either hardback or paperback books – very few sold both. The family firm of Penguin, founded by Allen Lane, had been bought by a larger group and, to combat the might of Penguin, three hardback publishers – Heinemann, Macmillan and Michael Joseph – had started their own jointly owned paperback company, Pan, which by the time I came on the scene was giving Penguin a run for its money under the leadership of Clarence Paget, with his brilliant sidekicks Sonny Mehta and Simon Master.

Hardback publishers sold the paperback rights in hardback books to paperback publishers and the powerful rights director – invariably a woman – would hold heated auctions between these paperback publishers, if the book was 'hot' enough.

Much of British publishing was quite parochial. But the arrival before the war of Jewish publishers fleeing Hitler's Europe had added spice in the form of the Neuraths at Thames & Hudson; Horowitz brought Phaedon from Vienna – where Weidenfeld came from; André Deutsch was from Budapest. These publishers had a much more international perspective. Deutsch had big success publishing North American writers like Norman Mailer, Philip Roth, J. K. Galbraith and Arthur Schlesinger, Europeans such as Simone de Beauvoir and Gitta Sereny, and Caribbean writers including V. S. Naipaul.

Many publishing deals were done over lunch – which was quite a bibulous event. Editors did not feel it necessary to consult their sales teams when they wanted to buy the rights to publish a book. Soon after I arrived at Curtis Brown, Graham Watson tipped the wink to his friends who duly issued invitations to lunch. I remember Sir Robert Lusty of Hutchinson – over wine in the Epicure in Charlotte Street – saying, 'Graham says you worked on the *Economist*. So you must know about figures and things. I remember when Michael Joseph and I founded Michael Joseph, he said to me one day: "Bob, what's turnover?"'

While some publishers were parochial, we agents were not. One of the appeals of the job to me was that I would be doing a lot of business in America. In his heyday, Graham Watson would visit New York for a month and see 120 editors while there. I would visit New York periodically to meet publishers and sell my wares – though usually on a two-week stint. And US editors would make annual visits to London for long stretches, and settle down in the Connaught, the Ritz or Browns for two or three weeks of seeing their authors and going round the offices of publishers and agents to pick up manuscripts. They would read the manuscripts in their hotel and then make offers to buy the rights. Nowadays we can offer a book by pinging the manuscript by email, so these visits are short.

———◇———

This was the world I entered in 1972. Graham Watson was my mentor. Every morning I would go in and sit with him and his secretary as he went through his mail and dictated a load of letters, all the time explaining their significance to me, the authors, editors or journalists involved, the nature of the deals, the details of the contracts. Graham had started his life in publishing before the war, so knew it from the inside. He spent the war in the Royal Artillery and joined Curtis Brown in 1947. His list of authors was distinguished, to say the least, including Daphne du Maurier, Hammond Innes, Elizabeth Longford, Wilfred Thesiger, Gore Vidal and the estates of John Steinbeck and Winston Churchill. I began to get the feel of the author–agent relationship. This was something that could last for decades. There was not much that Graham did not know about his authors. He had a wonderfully wry sense of humour and enjoyed telling stories of their antics.

I had inherited a small group of authors, most of whom wrote romantic fiction, of which I knew nothing. Before I met any of them, I had the luck of having lunch with Brenda Macdougal, the fiction editor of *Woman & Home*. I quizzed her like a journalist. Who were the big writers in this field, where did they sell, what was the short-story market like?

The fact was that with the arrival of television the bottom had fallen out of the short-story market. But magazines still needed at least one story an issue and the good writers could still sell. One of them she loved was Rosamunde Pilcher.

Recently, when she died at 94, I gave the tribute at Ros Pilcher's funeral and I remembered our first lunch together. I said:

Of all the qualities that spring to mind when I think of Ros I would say that listening was her first expertise. I was subtly grilled about my background in journalism, my Yorkshire family, my travels, all of which were of huge interest to her. When I paused for breath, she said: 'I bet you've never read Woman's Own!' *Years later, she told me that I had replied that it was never too late to start ...*

She then led me on a mystery tour of the ins and outs of romantic fiction publishing – in particular magazines, which were then her main source of income. She had close relationships with – and was much loved and admired by – the literary editors of Woman & Home, Woman's Own, Woman's Weekly, *etc. She knew exactly what they wanted and she delivered it. I could see she was a true professional who could teach me a lot.*

My first real stroke of luck was the arrival of Diana Crawfurd. She was a famous and glamorous agent who had begun her career working for a television agent and had snapped up a lot of the trendy TV personalities at that most trendy of times in the 60s, such as David Frost, Bamber Gascoigne and Christopher Booker. She had then started representing books and by the time I met her had an independent agency representing a star-studded list including Germaine Greer, Nigel Nicolson, James Pope-Hennessy, Shiva Naipaul and Frederick Forsyth. She happened to be romantically entangled with Nicholas Baring, brother of Susan Rogaly. So before I started at Curtis Brown, Joe and Susan invited me round to meet her.

I liked Diana a lot and she had encouraged me to join Curtis Brown and hinted, which was true, that they had approached her in the past with a view to buying her agency. So I was surprised that within months of my starting at Curtis Brown I bumped into Diana in King Street and she drew me aside, asking if I would be interested in jumping ship and joining her agency. It soon became clear the reason. She and Nicholas were getting married, she was in her mid-thirties and wanted to start having children and she needed more support. I had no wish to leave Curtis Brown, where I was feeling very treasured by Graham in particular, and I was not sure that with a powerful woman like Diana I would be able to develop independently as I planned.

The upshot was that Curtis Brown bought the Diana Crawfurd Agency, Diana moved into our premises, which were now in Craven Hill near Paddington, and we began to work quite closely together. Watching her in action was fascinating. Her authors clearly adored and relied on her and in most cases were very much part of her social life. Watching her strategising with them over lunch was a lesson in itself. Her world seemed to me ideal. When she did go off to have her first baby I did look after some of her authors, but luckily other Curtis Brown colleagues did too. The one I took on – and represented for the next 45 years – was John Julius Norwich.

In 2018 John Julius died aged 88. When I spoke at his memorial I remembered our first meeting:

In 1973 I was a novice literary agent. My starry colleague, Diana Baring, was off to have a baby. Would I look after John Julius? Round we went to Blomfield Road. WHAT a welcome he always gave! Over drinks – sparkling in every way – we hit it off.

John Julius was my ideal author. I love history and that was what he wrote. I learned so much from him. He was an exquisite writer. He relished the process, never happier than when cycling off for another day in his second home, the London library. He couldn't write a dull sentence. He wore his erudition so lightly – and he was such a pro. When we met, he was already deep into writing his magnum opus on Venice. But variety enthused him. There were TV series, *Round Britain Quiz*, lectures, travel pieces, and later he was founder-contributor of Classic FM, edited letters and of course he produced his annual *Christmas Cracker* commonplace collections.

He also thought like a journalist and was up for any new project. One November I received a call from someone at Mitchell Beazley – the publisher of detailed illustrated books, which they financed by pre-selling co-editions in many languages. 'We have this fantastic book, *Great Architecture of the World*: 1,000 illustrations, 100,000 words, big sales in Germany and the US. Delivery March. Only snag: no author ... I phoned John Julius. Could he be editor and front this project? He replied – not for the first or last time – 'My dear, it's the Money for Old Rope Department!'

At his study table we became a team, compiling a jaw-dropping list of contributors, many of whom had taught me at the Courtauld: Pevsner, Hugh Casson, Anthony Blunt, Michael Kitson. Everyone seemed happy to come on board. We put it to Elisabeth Brayne, the delightful editor at Mitchell Beazley. The book arrived on time and sold bucket-loads in 15 languages. That book led to me taking on more authors who were historians or art historians. It also led to the only disagreement that I had with Graham Watson.

In November 1979, Sir Anthony Blunt, former head of the Courtauld Institute, Keeper of the Queen's Pictures and general establishment figure, was revealed in Parliament to have been a spy for the Russians before and during the war. It was a mega scandal. Blunt went into hiding and the papers were full of it. A few days later, Graham came into my office and closed the door. 'George says that you represent Anthony Blunt' – George was our company secretary. Well, I explained, only up to a point. He had contributed the Baroque section to that big architecture book, which was why he was on our records. 'Well, if he approaches you with his memoirs you are not to take him on,' said Graham firmly.

Blunt had not approached me. But I said that to my generation a book that explained why it was that those highly educated upper-middle-class young men at Cambridge in the 30s like Burgess, Philby and Maclean had grasped the dogma of Communism so wholeheartedly would be very fascinating. We argued. But Graham was adamant. Finally, he said that I was not going to persuade him: 'I lived through the war and you did not. Curtis Brown will not make money out of traitors.' I found the conversation moving at the time – and I still do today.

One of the most successful matches that I made in the late 70s was for Rosamunde Pilcher. A man called Tom McCormack from St Martin's Press in New York would come to London twice a year with his big bag. He would tour the offices of agents and publishers and ask what you had for him. The temptation to sell a book to a publisher when he was sitting there was great. But in those days St Martin's was rather a wastepaper basket publisher – i.e. they bought books other publishers would not and paid a pittance for them. Then, just now and again – as in the case of James Herriott – one would hit the jackpot. But you did not sell to them if you could sell to Random House, Viking or Simon & Schuster.

So there I was in 1978 busily trying *not* to sell Tom a book. 'Anything you are particularly looking for?' I asked. 'Well, we are thinking of going into Romance,' he replied. 'Romance!' said I. 'You will love Rosamunde Pilcher.' I pointed to a line of old Pilcher titles, which had never been sold outside the UK. He put four in his bag, phoned me the next day and offered $1,000 each. Ros and I were over the moon. Her books did well, earning good royalties, and even got reviewed in the *New York Times* where the reviewer wrote: 'Rosamunde Pilcher. Where have you been all my life?' We sold more of the backlist to St Martin's and began to sell her short stories for $5,000 to *Good Housekeeping* magazine in New York and she built a following.

Some years later, Ros was going to see her daughter Pippa, who lived on Long Island. I suggested she should meet up with her young editor Tom Dunne, who I had met in New York. They duly had lunch together. He was captivated by Ros and he encouraged her to write longer novels, which she did and which sold better in Britain too. Then, en route to the Frankfurt Book Fair, Tom went to stay with Ros and her husband Graham in their home near Dundee in Scotland. Over drinks before dinner, Ros's son Robin bluntly asked: 'Why don't you sell more of Mother's books?' 'Because your mother doesn't write the right kind of books,' replied Tom. He told Robin that when he saw Ros, she told him the most amazing stories about her adventures and her life in the war when she had been a WREN in the Navy in Ceylon. But none of these excitements went into her books. 'If she could write me a door-stopper, which brought in these amazing experiences, that would be different.' Next morning after breakfast, Ros and Tom mapped out the plot of *The Shell Seekers*. Tom commissioned it for $25,000. It has now sold over 8 million copies in America and is in print in over 40 languages.

12.

Alasdair

When our boy Max was about five, he was strikingly bright and precocious. I remember someone saying that he was going to be brilliant. My reaction was instant: 'I don't want him to be brilliant,' I snapped. 'I want him to be bright enough to have an interesting life and career. Being brilliant is complicated.' I know that was because of Alasdair. Being married to a very brilliant man is difficult. Being a brilliant person who cannot decide what to do with his life makes you very restless. When Alasdair died aged only 48 in 1984, just before his book and television series on China, *The Heart of the Dragon*, was launched, the *Guardian* wrote: 'As a young man he was acknowledged as one of the most brilliant of his generation.'

I first met Alasdair at the ICA – the Institute of Contemporary Arts – which was a lively spot to hang out in the early 70s with its exhibitions, concerts and lectures and where Alasdair had performed folk concerts in the past. I was immediately struck by his sparkling conversation and he seemed such fun. He was also good-looking in a dark and interesting way. In my diary I put his address in January 1973 and we started seeing each other. In April – just before I headed off to travel with Larry in Haiti – we had a day walking in Hampstead together and then went to a concert at the Festival Hall given by his friend, the Iranian singer Shusha Guppy.

At that point he was working as a producer at the Open University, making films to accompany their courses. It was an interesting if low-profile job. But it suited him and was a good background against which he could work on all his other projects. While we were together he published a book on work, a book on the impact of television, a book of poems and a book of his folk songs and made a record of his songs. It was also, at 37, the first steady job he had had.

Alasdair was the son of a Danish doctor in Winchester and his English wife, Doris. He had two elder brothers, one of whom was a teacher married with children in Denmark and one an engineer, also married with children in Winchester. Alasdair had clearly been the star of the family and much adored by his mother, who was widowed quite young. He had been bright from the start and had got a scholarship to Winchester College, where he had been head boy, and then a scholarship to Oxford, where he had got a 'congratulatory' first in PPE and was then elected as a Prize Fellow at All Souls College. This fellowship was renewable every seven years and All Souls played a considerable part in his life.

He had clearly starred socially at Oxford and was close with eminent people like Isaiah Berlin, who had encouraged him to become an academic. He had rejected this idea, started training as an architect, dropped that and then somehow made a living as a writer of books and as a song-writer. He had had a number of steady girlfriends but had never managed to settle. I remember when we got together our mutual friend Peter Jay – who had been his friend at school and Oxford and was his rival for the All Souls Fellowship – described him as a Renaissance man who bemused him because he could never select a career path. In fact, Alasdair bemused many people.

He had lived in many places in London, including a barge at Limehouse near Jenny and Michael Barraclough (who have remained my friends ever since). But he was now settled in a flat he had bought at West Hill Court off Highgate West Hill. It was in a beautiful, four-storey 30s Art Deco block with views across Hampstead Heath. He was on the top floor with access to a great roof-garden area. He was clearly very pleased and happy with his flat.

With the exception of Nick and Connie Harman and Peter and Margaret Jay, we did not have close friends in common. But I enjoyed his friends, who I got to know that summer: Will and Veronica Plowden, who with their children were staying with the Harmans at their holiday house in Pembrokeshire when we visited in August. I have a picture of all their children packed into my tiny orange Honda, which had replaced my Mini at some point. I also met his great friends David and Clarissa Pryce Jones and Anthony and Eliane Grigg. Most of his friends were at the next stage in life, having married and had children, and saw Alasdair as something of a Peter Pan.

As our marriage ended so unhappily in late 1978 when I moved out (we finally divorced in 1981), I find it difficult to write about Alasdair. And it has been an interesting exercise going through my old diaries and photo albums and reminding myself that for a good length of time we were very happy. He was such an original person. He was very warm. You never quite knew what idea he would come up with next. I might arrive home from the office on a Friday and he would suggest we go to France for the weekend. We would leap on his scooter, take a train to some port and then have a happy weekend scooting around Honfleur – or wherever. We would go camping too – always taking a lot of his paperwork – for he was never not working on something.

Looking through my old letters, I found a number from Victoria Brittain from Saigon. She had parted from Andrew not long after their return from Washington. She and I saw a great deal of each other in the early 70s, and I would often drop by her house in Islington on my way home from work. It was in her basement kitchen in Gibson Square that I first met my life-long friend Roger Graef. In 1973, she pluckily decided to go with six-year-old little Casimir to Vietnam as a correspondent for *The Times*. I gave her a farewell party in my garden in Mayton Street and I have wonderful photos of the event with Victoria looking ravishing in a near see-through Indian garment. There is also a photo of Casimir with Alasdair. In her letters to me she responds to my letters, which were full of my doings with Alasdair. I was clearly very happy and enjoyed my involvement with his work.

And I was intrigued by his singing life. He had written many songs and also translated Jacques Brel, and his translations were sung by the likes of Judy Collins. My son Ben tells me his songs are still covered today; recently by the singer Feist. Faber Music had commissioned him to publish a collection of his songs, *Adam & the Beasts*, and so he made a record to accompany the book. His fellow singers were someone called Victoria (I don't know her other name) and the very wonderful young Emma Kirkby, who went on to become a very famous soprano. Emma singing folk songs is bewitching. Emma was married to the musician Andrew Parrott and they recorded the disc in a studio in Stonesfield near Oxford along with the composer Nick Bicât. The whole process was such fun – with baby Bicâts running about – and so interesting for me. I provided the jolly photograph of the team for the back of the record sleeve.

Alasdair was a dutiful son and I became very fond of his mother, Doris, who lived alone at Twyford near Winchester where her son Ian and family lived. She was clearly longing for Alasdair to settle down with me. So when finally we did decide to get married in that summer of 1973 she was aglow. It's worth mentioning that at some point before we got married I had thought that I had got pregnant. This alarmed me as I was not nearly ready for that. But Alasdair was quite excited and began talking about the children we might have. As it turned out, I was not pregnant. But it had given me the idea that when the time came, Alasdair would be an enthusiastic father.

We got married in November 1974 in the Crypt of the Houses of Parliament. It was a small wedding with our immediate families. Our bridesmaids were little Casilda Grigg, Alex Lankester, Rachel Rogaly and Becky Harman so all their families came, as did the Pryce Jones family as Clarissa took the splendid photographs. Muggs made me an exquisite creamy dress with a separate top (which changed to a pink version for the evening). This was very much the fashion of the time with designers like Gina Fratini. That evening we had a thumping great party for around

150 people in Hampstead's old Town Hall on Haverstock Hill. Lucilla helped me decorate it with woodland offerings – I remember yards of Old Man's Beard – and we danced away. We took an enchanting honeymoon on the Amalfi Coast south of Naples – visiting Pompeii, Herculaneum and Paestum – where the autumn sun made it beautiful and everything seemed to have emptied for us.

We then settled in West Hill Court. I did not sell Mayton Street. There was no need and the presence of a sitting tenant would make it difficult. So I let it. Later that autumn, Doris gave a party for us for her friends at Twyford and, after Christmas at Park Farm, my grandmother gave one for Yorkshire friends in Libby's Fulford house.

My diaries show a lively social life, staying with the Griggs at the glorious old family house at La Musclera near Barcelona; a trip to stay with Patrick and Clare with their baby Paddy in the Camargue – Patrick had taken a job there in order to keep his marriage together as Clare had left him once because she could not take the isolated life in the Serengeti with a little child. There were trips to Park Farm, which were better when there were lots of the family there at Christmas, and Alasdair got on really well with Annie and Emma. But my relationship with Cynthia was frosty. She did not like having to put up with her husband's children at Park Farm and clearly could not understand my father's pride in us – and this upset him a lot.

We loved visiting Spain. Our first trip was on an unbelievably cheap package tour to Benidorm. When we landed at Alicante airport the customs officers shrugged knowingly when our fellow travellers opened their suitcases to reveal Rice Krispies, Corn Flakes and corned beef – in fact anything to avoid Spanish food. When we arrived at our breeze-block high-rise hotel we were pretty appalled and the next day found us renting a motorbike and heading for the hills. It was just after Christmas when all was grim in England but the sun and the oranges were out. We stayed in a little inn and visited some enchanting white towns.

Some days later we re-joined our party at the Benidorm hotel to leave in a bus for the airport. It was New Year's Eve. On arrival we found our flight delayed and so we were destined to bring in the new year in the departure lounge. To make it worse there was loud background music, which Alasdair could not stand and made it impossible to socialise with our co-travellers. Alasdair disappeared and soon the music stopped. We then all started sharing our duty free, getting very jolly and singing the new year in. It was only later we discovered that by turning off the music system Alasdair had also turned off the loud-speaker system so our flight nearly left without us.

In late 1975 I visited South Africa for the first time. This was triggered by step-brother Alex, who was now working as an agricultural economist in Lesotho, having taken a postgraduate master's in the subject at Reading. But I was also intrigued to learn about South Africa under apartheid and the interesting literary scene that flourished there. Curtis Brown had a number of authors there including the legendary Mary Renault. Before leaving, I had been to talk to many of the South African exiles who lived in London. What I remember distinctly about our conversations, conducted in the gloom of autumn in North London, was how much they all loved and missed the land.

I flew to Johannesburg, where Alex met me, and we stayed with his cousin Andrew and his flatmate Bruce MacGregor. The MacGregors were old family friends of the Duncans from Cape Town days and Bruce arranged that when I visited Cape Town later in my journey I would stay with his parents, Alec and Jean. From Johannesburg we drove through the wide plains of the Free State to cross the border into Lesotho and then north to Leribe where Alex lived. I began to understand that feel for the land. Seeing the mountains of Lesotho rising in the distance from the flat plain is an exhilarating sight.

My visit was very happy. Alex had good local friends and I remember a wonderful day when we drove hours up a dirt road into the mountains to visit his friend, a charming farmer called Dai Molapo. As Alex was working during the week, I took a car and drove over the border and went south to stay with an author I represented called Daphne Olivier, who wrote crime novels under a male pseudonym. The journey around the Drakensberg was terrific. She lived in Natal, near Pietermaritzburg, and was married to an Afrikaner farmer. This was a blind date and all the more fascinating for that because this was my first encounter with an Afrikaner.

They were enormously hospitable family people. Their rose farm interested me a lot. I really enjoyed my visit. But the memorable conversation was on my last night sitting around the fire after the braai, when Mr Olivier told me about his grandmother. She had been an Englishwoman from Woking who had come out in the late nineteenth century to South Africa as a nanny to an English family who were coming to work there. Once she arrived, it became clear that nanny jobs were done by black people. But she stayed and in due course she met an

Afrikaner farmer, married him, learned Afrikaans, settled on the farm in northern Natal and had some children.

Then came the Boer War. It began in 1899. But the scorched earth policy – whereby the British army took the old people, women and children from their farms and confined them in 'concentration' camps and torched their homes so they could not supply the guerrilla fighters – came later. When the British soldiers arrived at her farm, they realised she was English and suggested they take her elsewhere. But she said: 'I will go with my people.' It is estimated that around 26,000 people died of typhoid or other diseases in those camps. It was a scandal revealed by the famous Emily Hobhouse in *The Times*, which caused uproar in Britain.

His grandmother witnessed and lived through this horror in a camp but survived. She felt outrage and shame at the British, her fellow country-men. After the war, she returned to the burnt-out farm and reunited with her husband. Then this English woman made a vow: no word of English would ever pass her lips again. So when my host, as a young man, came to introduce his English-speaking fiancée from the very English town of Durban to his grandmother, the old lady welcomed her in Afrikaans and for the rest of her life never spoke to Daphne in English.

The way my host told me this story made me think of Northern Ireland. I had visited Belfast that year to stay with John Graham when he was the FT correspondent there and I remember him talking about how in Ireland people talked of historical events as if they had witnessed them themselves – a true feeling of history being part of your daily life. I felt it was helpful in understanding the Afrikaner mind-set. When I finally got to Johannesburg, the liberal intellectuals I met were visibly surprised that I had stayed with an Afrikaner.

After another day with Alex, I flew from Bloemfontein to Cape Town. I can still see my welcoming, elegant hostess Jean MacGregor, with her mass of white hair and her black coat, waiting for me at the airport. She was a heavenly woman. We drove to her house, Suddie, in a beautiful suburb called Tokai. We had instantly taken to each other, and I also liked her charming, rather quieter husband, Alec. Next day she took me around this spacious area with its ravishing gardens and showed me much of downtown Cape Town. Jean had a brilliant, artistic eye and her house was decorated with such flair and care. When I visit her daughter Mim, who later became a great friend, I see that same flair in her home in Constantia.

I had already made appointments with publishers and writers so I knew I was going to have a fascinating few days. On my second evening, Jean said, 'I'm sure Cynthia has given you lots of introductions.' 'No, she hasn't, but I'll be fine,' I replied. She looked me straight in the eye. 'Is she as vile to you as she was to the Duncans?' I replied that it had not been easy. She went on: 'Cynthia is one of my greatest friends. We had wonderful times with her and our children. We all so admired the way she kept the family together and coped when Patrick was so tied up in his politics. But the way she treated her husband's family had to be seen to be believed. It was as if a devil got into her.'

The feeling of relief was enormous. I could not wait to tell my father and Libby and Bunny. It was not our fault. We had all wondered where we had gone wrong. Jean went on to say that Cynthia had particular difficulty with women who her husband loved. As far as she was concerned, it could only be jealousy, pure and simple as that. 'She got on fine with Pat's brother John until he produced his young wife, Pam, who

Patrick loved.' Cynthia had always been very cold with Pam and with Patrick's sister Deb. I mentioned that Cynthia had told my father she hated seeing him kiss women when he greeted them – something he could not stop doing with old family friends but which troubled her.

Jean and I had many engrossing conversations. I heard a lot about her children and about their lives with which she was so deeply involved. On my last day there, I went for a walk in the woods behind the house and found myself crying my heart out. Jean had made me realise just how much I missed having a mother; someone who would continue to be involved in your life long after you stopped being a child. I had lost that relationship in my teens.

Years later in 1987, Jean was visiting me in Kidlington just after our younger boy Ben was born. She said that her daughter Mim, who lived in Zimbabwe, was expecting a baby and she was concerned that it would have a South African passport – which at the time of apartheid was a great disadvantage. I offered to have Mim to stay so she could have the baby in Oxford. This happened. For several months Mim lived in our house, had her baby, Ian, who is now aged 32, and we became friends for life.

One memorable meeting when in Cape Town was with Mary Renault – who at that time was an enormously successful novelist with her books on ancient Greece, which I had devoured. Before leaving London, her agent Juliet O'Hea told me a lot about her but mentioned in passing that, while they regularly wrote each other long letters, they had never met. Mary had read English at Oxford and then trained as a nurse at the Radcliffe Infirmary. There she became romantically involved with a fellow nurse, Julie Mullard. During the war she started writing contemporary novels and was represented by Spencer Curtis Brown. In 1945 she had won a huge award for *Return to Night*, which had enabled her and Julie to emigrate to South Africa, where there was an ex-pat gay community among which they felt more at home. They had never returned to England.

Now they were living along the coast in Hermanus and I rented a little red Volkswagen and headed there. We had a delightful time. We sat on the stoep of their cosy bungalow while Julie served tea and Mary asked a great deal about London and editors she dealt with – there was a lot about what everybody looked like. Mary explained that Juliet had become her agent when Mary had produced her first Greek novel *The Last of the Wine*. Spencer had pronounced it good but not commercial and had encouraged her to write another nursing romance. She was dutifully doing this when *The Last of the Wine* became an international bestseller. Spencer apologised and suggested that perhaps a new, younger agent might suit her better.

The chat went on and suddenly Mary said, 'Just think, Julie. It's Thursday and here we are enjoying ourselves with Felicity without a care in the world.' What, I asked, was so special about Thursday? On Thursday, they explained, they used to have their hair done. It was all such a palaver parking in Hermanus and took up the whole morning. 'So we decided we had had enough. And here we are wearing wigs!'

After Cape Town, I flew to Plettenberg Bay along the West Cape coast where John and Pam Duncan were expecting me. Jean had phoned ahead and told them about our Cynthia conversation so no explanations were necessary. I felt incredibly welcomed. John had had a career in the book trade working for CNA, the big South African book chain. But he had taken early retirement and with his payoff had started a bookshop. He and Pam had gone into business with a Greek family who wanted to start a restaurant. They had bought land in Plett along the main street and built a pleasant-looking shopping centre with flats above it with the restaurant at one end and the bookshop at the other. It had been going a year or more and so far was flourishing. Pam and John had not worked together before and were clearly enjoying it.

They had a charming house with a good-sized garden bang in the centre of town but had longer-term plans to build some houses outside town with Pam's brothers. This in fact happened and in the 90s Alex and I and our children spent some great holidays at Trinity Farm. I loved spending time with Pam and John. They were so very warm and interesting and of course it was fascinating for me to find out a great deal more about the Duncan family. They loved Alex and I remember Pam saying that 'when Alex laughs he reminds me so much of Pat'. And of course we had the book trade in common. Until his death, I always had marvellous conversations with John about the books he was reading.

Back in Johannesburg I met publishers and authors, had an evening with Nadine Gordimer, lunch with Barney Simon, the playwright, and generally got to find out something of the cultural scene. But it was all very white. My contact with black people had all been in a servant capacity. And I remember looking at the huge and rich city of Johannesburg, with its skyscrapers and signs of prosperity, and thinking that the apartheid regime was too powerful and that things would never change without a revolution.

In October 1975, I had hit 30. We had a party at our flat in West Hill Court and I remember, rather smugly, feeling very happy to be me. There I was, married to this fascinating man, having wonderful friends, looking good and being successful in my ever-varied job. And things certainly continued so for several years. At some point Alasdair got a job as a reporter on a Sunday-night TV current affairs programme. He did well on it but overall it was not a success and was clearly not going to be repeated. It was only then that he realised that he could not get his job at the Open University back.

Having to go freelance again did not suit him. He soon got a job working on the *Economist*, but that did not last long. The timing was very bad. I remember on one of our visits to Spain we visited my mother's grave outside Marbella. The effect on me was quite startling. We began to talk about having children and it was clear that he did not want to at all. Our flat would not be a child-friendly place. We had disagreements about the possibility of moving. I began to resent the fact that he spent so many weekends in Oxford – All Souls was more important to him now that he did not have a regular job.

Just going over that period in my mind makes me sad. I know that by the time we went to Boulder, Colorado, for Howard Higman's annual conference in spring 1978, there were problems between us and I remember confiding them to my new friend, the writer Leslie Garis, who was attending the conference with her playwright husband Arthur Kopit. I remember meeting Leslie at a party on our first night in Boulder and thinking: 'I want to be your friend.' Alasdair felt the same with both her and Arthur and long after we parted we both kept up with them. By September of 1978 I had moved out and back to Mayton Street.

September 1978 was the month that Libby married Ronald Higgins. I had always felt they would be suited but my first efforts did not work. I had invited them to dinner together back in 1972 and Ronald later said that while he fancied her he could not see where he would fit into her ever-so-busy schedule ... Libby's enthusiasms for what she was up to could be at times exhausting. Then of course he had had his time with Bunny, which ended sadly. He had lost his job on the *Observer* but had then written a remarkable book called *The Seventh Enemy* about the threats to civilisation as we know it – which today seems extremely prescient.

His agent for the book was my colleague Peter Grose, who had a country place near Ronald in Herefordshire. I remember being in New York and on the phone to Peter. 'I saw your sister Libby last weekend,' he said. 'She was staying with Ronald Higgins. They seemed very happy together.' You could have knocked me over with a feather. Quickly I phoned Libby and did indeed find her euphoric. She was clearly in love at last and couldn't stop talking about it. When I put the phone down I paused. What must Bunny be thinking? So I lifted the phone to her. 'I have just heard about Libby and Ronald,' I said. 'You must feel pretty odd.' 'Yes, Fliss, I do,' she said in that very gentle voice. 'But I am happy for them.'

Alasdair did not come to the wedding. From then on we saw each other sporadically. I became involved with another man and Alasdair had a girlfriend. In 1981 Leslie Garis was staying with me from the US. She went and spent an evening with Alasdair. She came back very excited. He had just heard that the project that he and his friend Peter Montagnon had been working on for several years had got the go-ahead. They were to make a ten-part series on contemporary China for the newly founded Channel 4. Alasdair would be a producer on the series and write the accompanying book, *The Heart of the Dragon*. I was thrilled for him. This would mark an end to his insecurities. Antelope Films was up and running.

Over the next few years Alasdair worked on that series and on the book. It was to be launched in January 1984. Then in October 1983 I was in hospital having just given birth to mine and Alex's second child, Max. Alex brought my post into the hospital and there was a copy of the *Bookseller* with the vibrant jacket design of Alasdair's book on the front cover. I wrote to him from hospital saying how pleased I was for him. I also told him that I had just had a little boy.

Days later I was back at home in the ramshackle Old Rectory in Kidlington we had only moved into in June. It was a Sunday and Alex was out but my friend Susan Brigden, Max's godmother, was with me and our oldest child, Alice, who was 16 months old. I was in my dressing gown and we were sitting in my bedroom. The doorbell rang and there was Alasdair. He had got my letter and wanted to give his good wishes. He came to join us upstairs and see baby Max and Alice. He asked to see the house. So I took him around the chaotic dusty rooms full of boxes and builders' tools. We were going to divide the house and let off a large part to pay our mortgage. It didn't look too inviting. 'This could have been us,' he said. I said it certainly could not. Restoring an old rectory complete with deathwatch beetle was the last thing that my Peter Pan-like former husband would have relished. But he was adamant.

It became an obsession. He would phone me daily – sometimes going on for nearly an hour. He had all kinds of worries that only I could resolve. His American girlfriend had left and I was the only person he could talk to. He was worried about the reception to his book, about a speeding fine. But above all seeing me with the children had made him realise what he had lost. And so it went on. He was clearly mentally unwell and I told him he should see a psychiatrist. Finally, one time Alex picked up the phone. He asked Alasdair not to call again. I was tired and it was upsetting for me.

In January, I was back from maternity leave and sitting in my office in London. Alasdair phoned. He sounded much calmer. He wanted to reassure me that he had heard that he had not lost his driving licence. And things were going well with the launch of the *Heart of the Dragon* TV series. It was a friendly conversation and I was relieved. A few days later Peter Montagnon phoned me at the office. Alasdair was dead. He had thrown himself under a train at Kentish Town tube station the night before.

Of course I was shocked, but in truth not surprised. And the horror was that he was on his own and it was I who had to break the news to his mother. She stood in his study holding two bags of groceries. 'But I've got his supper,' she said. He was buried in Winchester and I arranged a memorial at St James's Church, Piccadilly, at which there were moving speeches. But the most heart-rending was hearing Emma Kirkby singing 'Hawthorne Berries', which they had sung together on his record *Adam & the Beasts*.

13.

My Life with Gardening

R ecently I started regaling our wonderful neighbours Brad Cohen and Brona O'Toole about the launch of the Felicity Bryan chrysanthemum. It brought back so many memories of my four years as Gardening Correspondent of the *Evening Standard* – an unlikely posting but one that brought such variety and joy to my life and led to a lifelong involvement in the world of garden writers.

It started like this. In 1975, Simon Jenkins was features editor of the *Evening Standard*. As such, he was always looking for writers for pieces and I would enjoy supplying the cook to replace Delia Smith when she went on holiday, and so on. One day he said they were looking for a weekly gardening correspondent to replace the chief sub who had been doing it since time immemorial and was retiring. I threw him some names. He turned them down. The applicant must be a Londoner who understood the challenges of London gardening. They were thinking of holding a competition. 'Why don't you apply?' 'Well, as you know, I'm a passionate gardener but I don't know enough.' 'I think you know enough to start,' he said.

He had put a bee in my bonnet. The following weekend I sat down and wrote three 500-word pieces – I only remember that one was on roses – and sent them to Simon. If that worked, I thought I could do it in the time allowed. He gave them to Trevor Grove, who had now taken on the features role, and Trevor took me on for a month's trial. I loved it.

Writing a weekly column is surprisingly easy. You collect ideas all the time. No information is un-useful. My filing system of ideas began to grow. Then at 6.00 every Tuesday morning I would sit down and type my 500 words, have it done by 8.00 a.m. then post it to Trevor to appear on Delia's page the following Friday. Until I started doing it, I had not realised how much I had missed writing regularly. It keeps your ear attuned.

To improve my knowledge I bought books. But I also headed off to a weekly evening class held at William Ellis School just down Highgate West Hill from our flat in Millfield Lane – I used my married name, Felicity Clayre, to disguise the usurper. I had never attended an evening class before and loved the whole procedure. My fellow students were various, but we were united in our love of gardening. Our teacher was a spry, elderly man called – you guessed it – Mr Garlick, who tooled in from Eltham. I still have his excellent notes somewhere and learned a lot of basic stuff. And of course the questions from the students and the conversations in the break – where we sat on round tables with our teacher, often listening in to parallel animated talk on the neighbouring tables where courses in choux pastry or German opera were being discussed – were all grist to my mill. On several occasions I remember someone saying, 'That girl on the *Standard* said we should try X, or Y.'

And of course writing the column made me garden more. Alasdair's flat in West Hill Court had a huge roof terrace running the length of the building with a pergola. We had large tubs in which we grew climbing roses, honeysuckle, passion flowers, etc. and bedding plants and bulbs. I now added a plastic greenhouse, hoping that my readers could have at least some space under glass to grow seedlings, tomatoes and peppers. Meanwhile, I still owned my old Holloway house in Mayton Street with its 20-foot garden where the tenants were only too happy for me to toil. So that became my allotment. This way subject matter was never short.

It also made me travel. Often a weekend would be spent visiting Nymans and Sissinghurst in May, Kew in June, and National Trust gardens within easy reach of London. I got to know the gardeners and owners of these properties like Rosemary Verey at Barnsley House and Christopher Lloyd at Great Dixter – two of my heroes.

And I got to know the gardening press. There were lots of junkets to visit seed trials, rose growers and so on, and I particularly remember a very wet day when we went on buses to visit the gardens that were to feature in a TV series on garden history. Our bus got stuck at Beckley Park – an amazing fifteenth-century house, little changed except for a garden which was famed for its topiary. As the rain pelted down, we were entertained by the Feildings – the owners – and Mrs Feilding's sister, who regaled us on the subject of her wedding night: 'You young things are so worldly now. We did not know a thing. When my nanny and I were putting my trousseau together she said: "You must remember to sew fur around the bottom of your nightgown." I asked, "Why should I sew fur around the bottom of my nightgown?" And she said: "To keep your neck warm."' This was the first indication she had received that anything untoward would happen on her wedding night.

Among the gardening press was Ken, the night news editor of the *Mail*, who also helped with Percy Thrower's column. He was much liked and we really got on well, often exchanging Fleet Street gossip. It was with him that I got my own chrysanthemum. The venue was the press launch of the RHS Great Autumn Show – a brilliant event held every September in the Great Halls in Vincent Square. I loved the autumn colours – the hips and glowing Michaelmas daisies, the dahlias. With wine glasses in hand, Ken and I were passing the stand of Mr and Mrs Hall, breeders of prize-winning chrysanthemums and also on the tipple. 'That's a fine-looking new one,' said Ken. 'What's it called?' It did not have a name yet. So far it was just numbers. By the time we had left, the Halls had named one plant after Ken and one after myself.

Come next spring the Hall catalogue landed on the mat introducing Felicity Bryan and describing her as: 'A lively sport. Best to nip out in May ...' Nipping out means reducing the number of flower buds so that those remaining grow much bigger – some might say gross. Left to her own devices, Felicity Bryan was a very pretty soft, deep rosy colour with a mass of medium-sized flowers. My grandmother bought quantities of them for her neighbours in Fulford. Nipped out, her flower became huge and began to look like an old-fashioned petal bathing hat and not nearly so attractive. I attended my first chrysanthemum show at the RHS hall to see Felicity unveiled. I was fascinated to see the clientele. There were none of the pin-stripe-suited gentlemen and elegant women who attend the rose shows. It was all flat caps and jackets, mostly from the

In my house in Mayton Street, Holloway

Portrait of an agent

With author Mary Benson

With author Rosamunde Pilcher

Bunny, Muggs (Margaret Beale), my father and my grandmother Mardy. Fulford, York

My father in about 1979

With Alex in the Gambia, Christmas 1980

Marriage to Alex, October 1981

In my wedding dress, 1981

With Alex, Alice, Max and Ben in our garden in Kidlington

With Caroline Wood, Catherine Clarke and Carrie Plitt at Felicity Bryan Associates office

At a party in 2015 (photo by Harry Sherwood)

north – very much the sort of men you would expect to grow prize leeks and onions. There was class-consciousness even in the plant world.

Of course once I was meeting gardening writers I realised how poorly they were treated by many publishers when they wrote books, so I saw an opportunity. In time I became the go-to agent for gardening writers. I think John Brookes was the first. He had changed the way people thought about garden design with his book *A Room Outside* (1969). Dorling Kindersley had said they were looking for a garden designer. John had been paid an outright fee for his *The Small Garden*, which had been an international bestseller. With DK I could get him a decent deal with royalties and many more books followed.

An early client was Penelope Hobhouse. She had sent me her first book, *The Country Gardener* (1976), and I had read it and thought her a very good and knowledgeable writer. I can still see her sitting in my office at Curtis Brown in her smart tweeds. I was not excited. She was clearly a well-off country lady living in her famous Hadspen House in Somerset with its glorious garden and did not need the money. Nor did she have an idea for her next book. Time passed and then by chance a publisher from Heinemann mentioned to me that Gertrude Jekyll was going out of copyright. I immediately suggested Penny could do an anthology from the many Jekyll books, which she adored. Penny leapt at the idea.

We met up at Heinemann in Mayfair and Penny had invited me to lunch at her flat in Pimlico afterwards. The meeting with the publisher went well and then I offered Penny a lift to her flat as I had parked my car in front of the door. She looked quite put out. Her car was in the underground car park at Marble Arch. I would reach her flat first but someone would be there. That someone turned out to be a distinguished-looking gentleman doctor called John Malins. He gave me a drink and made me welcome and started discussing the meeting at the publishers, which he clearly knew all about. Then Penny arrived looking flustered. 'Ah, you have met John. You see, Felicity, I live with John during the week and my husband at weekends! Phew!!'

We had a delightful lunch. She and John were clearly soul mates. They had met through a Garden History Society tour and had fallen head over heels in love. In her early fifties, Penny was positively skittish. Clearly the arrangement of weekends at Hadspen could not last and soon Penny left her husband. I remember when that happened several gardeners saying to me: 'How *could* she leave that garden?' – not 'How could she leave her husband?' For a while John and Penny lived in London. Then, happily, the National Trust needed a new person to run Tintinhull Garden in Somerset. John and Penny moved there and had an extraordinarily productive and happy period together, when I would visit quite regularly, until John's death in 1992.

Recently Alex and I went to celebrate Penny's ninetieth birthday and I reminisced about that time. There is no doubt that, as Penny said, I suddenly took much more interest in her once she had left her husband and needed to earn some money. Not only did I fix book contracts for her, but also through my *Evening Standard* contacts I found myself recommending Penny for garden design jobs. I remember being pleased to get her a London square.

The 80s and the 90s were the heyday of garden publishing. The publisher Frances Lincoln blazed the trail for the exquisite-looking, heavily illustrated but informative book of which she could sell quantities of copies to publishers in the US and in many languages. Penny's *Colour in Your Garden* (1986) was just such a book. She went on writing books for the next 20 years with huge success.

It was her great friend Rosemary Verey – also an enormously influential and successful gardener with her amazing creations at Barnsley House in Gloucestershire – who introduced Penny to the US gardening lecture circuit on which Rosemary was a veteran. American gardeners loved these learned but aristocratic ladies, and Penny and Rosemary both designed gardens in America and in Europe. Rosemary had approached me to be her agent and I had agreed on condition that Penny was happy as there was potential competition. There was never a problem as they were good friends and both far too busy to worry about the other getting jobs.

Rosemary had made her name with *The Englishwoman's Garden*: the idea of the brilliant Sebastian Walker – when he was an editor at Chatto and before he went off to found the innovative Walker Books. It consisted of essays on different gardens by the women who gardened them, all edited by Rosemary and her friend Alvilde Lees Milne. The jacket displayed a heart-stopping picture of Rosemary's inspired Laburnum Walk at Barnsley House. The book was a spring bestseller, which sold on through Christmas. The only snag was that the editors had done it for an outright fee. I took over and got them a proper deal for the sequel and had the pleasure of looking after Rosemary for her many books until she died in 2001 aged 82. Rosemary was very firm about her garden ideas but she also had enormous charm and style. She designed gardens for an eclectic and international clientele, which included Prince Charles and Elton John, who both adored her.

Sometime in the 80s I wrote a piece for the *Guardian* about women gardeners. I included Rosemary and Penny. What these women had in common was that – being the generation they were – they had married young and settled down to motherhood early, not having a career path despite the fact that they both had good degrees. Both of them had taken to gardening after their children had got older or left the nest. I felt that it used the same nurturing instincts. And for both of them it gave them a stunning career in middle age. I, being another generation, had taken to gardening instead of having children. The irony was that once I did have children and had a big garden I was too taken up with the little ones. I did not feel the garden drawing me out, as it had in my youth.

Roy Strong, with his wife, the theatre designer Julia Trevelyan Oman, had created an extraordinary and extremely theatrical garden in Herefordshire on a plot of 23 acres. I love their house – the Laskett. It is so much *not* the kind of garden I would want, as Roy and Julia could not stop changing it. There was never any sitting back; always a change of scene. I already represented Roy for his history books and I introduced him to Alison Cathie of Conran Octopus, who was a genius at putting illustrated co-productions together. Between them she and Roy planned a series of enchanting books which used Roy's natural talent for design and invention in a wonderfully accessible way.

And then there was Mirabel Osler. When Rosemary Verey said I should represent her I said I already had enough gardening authors. 'But she is different. She is a poet.' Rosemary gave me articles that Mirabel had written for *Hortus* magazine. They were indeed poetic and inspiring. Her first book, *A Gentle Plea for Chaos*, was described by the *New York Times* as 'a blast of fresh air through the stuffy rooms of the English gardening world' and is pure pleasure to read. It describes how she created a garden in Herefordshire with her husband Michael when they returned from living in Thailand. Tragically, Michael died before the book was published. I loved Mirabel. She was so original and excited by life. Her books had a whole new following. I remember my first visit to her garden: she handed me a glass of wine, put it on a tray suspended from a tree, climbed the tree and then drew up our drinks.

The pleasure of representing all these gardening writers was enormous. They all became great friends and enticed me into a world that did not seem at all like work. However, the biggest commercial success I had was with a man who wanted to write about snowdrops ... Chris Brickell is a distinguished botanist and horticulturalist who was director of the Royal Horticultural Society. I had met him and we had had lunch to talk about book ideas. He said, 'What I really want to do is write a book about snowdrops. There is so, so much to say about snowdrops.' Wearing my commercial hat, I could not see this.

Fast forward some years and I read in 1984 that Robin Herbert, a bigwig in the City and keen plantsman, was becoming chairman of the RHS. I wrote to him saying that I felt the RHS could be more involved with books and I would love to help. The result was a meeting with Robin and two rather musty-looking men at the RHS offices in Vincent Square. I suggested that the RHS could lend its name to a series of books, which I could initiate with a publisher. Many distinguished writers would want to be involved. The potential was enormous. But whatever I suggested was turned down. I remember coming back to the office where my assistant asked how the meeting went. 'It was the sort of meeting that made me want to emigrate,' I said.

Then one day I was at Dorling Kindersley talking with Christopher Davies, the inspired editor and my great friend. He mentioned that they were planning a major encyclopaedia of plants and flowers and had approached the RHS to see if they could be involved and lend their brand. They had been rejected as the RHS said that they only put their name on something that had already been written and that they had approved. I got in touch with Robin Herbert and we met for supper. I said the RHS was mad to turn down this opportunity. DK would produce a brilliant book, investing huge sums in it, and after that nobody would do such a thing again for 20 years – and the RHS would have missed the opportunity to make a lot of money. 'I think this book could sell 100,000 copies,' I said. 'You could get over the problem of approval by putting one of your people in as the overall editor. How about Chris Brickell?'

So, to cut a long story short, this was finally approved. I did the deal with the RHS and DK. Chris worked like a slave putting that book together with the team at DK. The magnificent-looking book was published in 1989. It was followed by *The RHS Encyclopaedia of Gardening* and *The RHS A–Z of Plants and Flowers*. Thirty years, and many editions, on, *The Gardeners' Encyclopaedia of Plants and Flowers* has sold well over three million copies.

14.

Authors

Sometimes when people ask me about my job they ask how many authors I represent. And of course it's a difficult question. Because the number means nothing. A very busy and successful full-time writer will take up a great deal of your time. As their agent you are generally helping them orchestrate their life: managing the sales of UK and US rights and of translation rights in their books in many languages; arranging appearances, lectures, etc.; selling film rights. But you can represent an academic who produces a book every five years and takes up very little of your time. Novelists can go to ground for years. But because they work on their own, they usually want regular chats if only to keep them sane.

Roy Strong is a good example of an author who took up very little time but then became a full-time writer. I remember him, director of the Victoria and Albert Museum, calling me in 1986. I had represented him for some time and was, with my Courtauld Institute background, an appropriate agent as we spoke the same art-historical language. But there had never been much for me to do as he was so busy with his job. We sat in his elegant office at the V&A – decor courtesy of his wife, Julia – and he made a dramatic declaration. 'I am retiring and' – pointing at me in a severe way – 'from now on I am relying on *you* for my income.' It was a complete surprise. He was 51. Roy had been the *enfant terrible* of the art world, becoming the director of the National Portrait Gallery at 32 and the V&A at 38. He had been responsible for ground-breaking exhibitions. But he felt the time had come.

Suddenly I had to roar into action. Roy is a workaholic. He always requires to have at least one book on the go and to know what will be the next one. There was a magical one on Cecil Beaton, called *The Royal Portraits*, the first of four volumes of highly entertaining and scurrilous *Diaries*, books on gardening, portraiture and so on. We were never still.

Years later, one of the things I enjoyed most was *The Story of Britain*. My daughter Alice had, aged six, expressed an interest in history. I had gone to Blackwell's to find *Our Island Story* by H. E. Marshall – the book that had introduced me to history as a child. 'Everyone asks for *Our Island Story*,' said the lady in the children's section. 'It's out of print and there is no other narrative history – the history books for kids are all done in spreads for topic work.' Here was an opportunity. I got hold of an ancient copy of *Our Island Story* through a book search – this is pre-Abe Books – and told my friend Tricia Lankester – by now head of History at a comprehensive school in London – that I planned to get it re-issued. 'I think you will find it will not work today,' she cautioned.

Of course she was right. It is imperialist, sexist and racist. But it does tell a rattling good yarn.

I phoned Roy for advice. I knew that he and Julia were not interested in children but he might suggest another historian. He said he would think about it. Next thing I knew I was being bombarded with chapters – I distinctly recall one on Bess of Hardwick. Roy loved the idea and agreed there was a gap in the market for a big narrative history from the Celts to Mrs Thatcher. It took us a while to find a publisher: children's publishing did not seem to be versatile and this did not hit the school curriculum. But in due course the legendary Julia Macrae, who had her own children's book list at Random House, embraced the idea. *The Story of Britain* – all 600 lavishly illustrated pages of it – was published in 1996 and sold well over 100,000 copies. It is still in print today.

In the mid-70s, when I was writing my gardening column, I became friendly with Delia Smith with whom I shared a page on Fridays. We would compare notes on things like tomatoes and periodically cross-refer. One day Delia phoned me. She had this friend called Mary Berry. 'She does what I do but on ITV.' Mary at that point was the cook on *Good Afternoon* – a programme on Thames Television with Judith Chalmers. She had been ill-served by Hamlyn, whose *All Colour Cookbook* she had written the lion's share of for an outright fee. She needed an agent. 'But I can't send her to mine as we are too alike. You know, our recipes work ...' I met Mary and we got on right away. She was so warm and straight-forward and professional – and also fun.

We kicked off with books tied in with her TV series but then branched out. I lose count of how many books Mary has written now. But the one I feel most proud of is Dorling Kindersley's *Mary Berry's*

Complete Cookbook. My friend Christopher Davies was looking for someone to write a big 'complete' book, which they would publish with *Good Housekeeping* in the US. I suggested Mary. 'I think she's a bit old-fashioned,' he replied – male chefs with spiky hair were all the rage at that time. I told him to go back to the office and ask his colleagues which cook they and their mothers trusted most. He came back to me. I was right. They all agreed Mary Berry. I phoned Mary in triumph. But no. She did not want to publish with DK. She had had an unsatisfactory experience in the past. 'Grit your teeth for a year, Mary,' I said. 'I promise you that you will have a better experience. And this will be your pension. You will be crying all the way to the bank.' That book has now sold over two million copies.

When on the *Economist* I became friends with Richard Casement, who was the first science editor. He had persuaded Andrew Knight, the editor, that they needed a science section as a popular science cover always sold heavily off news-stands. There was clearly a growing market for this and it was one that I wished to explore in books. When Francis Crick – he who had won the Nobel Prize with Watson for discovering the structure of DNA – approached me, I said my problem was that I was scientifically illiterate. To this he replied, 'Well, that's the point. My feeling was that if you could understand it, anybody could.' So I represented Francis for *Life Itself*, which became an international bestseller and he was the first of many writers on science that I took on.

Francis was a colourful character. I vividly remember weekending with him and his wife, Odile, in a cottage outside Cambridge. I parked the car and walked down a rose-draped pergola. My host walked gleefully towards me wearing nothing but a straw hat. That was just the way he was.

Years later, I visited Francis and Odile in California and, after he died, I was thrilled that I persuaded my old friend James Atlas to commission Matt Ridley to write his excellent and succinct biography of Francis in the Harper Lives series.

In 1979, to our surprise, Peter Grose said he was leaving Curtis Brown to become a publisher at Secker & Warburg. The authors he represented tended to be male thriller writers or adventurers and not my cup of tea. So when Graham Watson came into my office and asked if I would be interested in any of Peter's authors I said: 'Only one. And that's Gerry Durrell. And if you don't give me Gerry I might just walk out.' Gerry Durrell had been a hero of mine since I had read *My Family and Other Animals* as a child. The Durrells – Larry and Gerry – were both long-time authors of Curtis Brown and their antics part of the folklore. It was agreed that I should go to visit Gerry at his zoo in Jersey to get his approval.

Before I headed off, Peter briefed me. It was not encouraging. Gerry was a busted flush. His books were not selling in the way they had, and he was drinking far too heavily. All his efforts went in to raising money for the Jersey Wildlife Trust – his zoo that he had founded on the island. It was true that since his recent marriage to Lee, his lifestyle had improved. But I was clearly inheriting an author on the wane. And one thing I know: when an author gets a new agent he expects things to look up. So off I flew to Jersey.

Imagine my surprise when I was greeted by my jolly host who told me proudly that he was on the wagon. The next surprise was Lee. She was my generation and we got on immediately. She was sparkling, brilliant and beautiful. Their story went like this: Gerry had been married for many years to Jackie – who featured in some of his earlier books. But Jackie had left him after over 20 years and – to add insult to injury – had gone off with a woman. For an alpha male like Gerry this was extra upsetting. What's more, because she had not run off with a man the law said she could still get alimony, which Gerry deeply resented. Durrells have always been drinkers. But these events drove Gerry into an extremely bad patch.

Then in 1977, when Gerry was on his annual fund-raising jaunt in America, he was visiting Duke University, North Carolina. One evening he met a sparkling young animal behaviourist called Lee McGeorge, who he immediately took to. Next day he asked her boss about her. His enthusiasm brimmed: she was brilliant; her thesis on birdsong in Madagascar was exceptional; she would go far. So Gerry sought her out. The Wildlife Trust did a lot of work in Madagascar, particularly on lemurs. And by chance they had a scholarship at the zoo whereby they invited a graduate student to come every year and spend the summer working there in Jersey. He could guarantee nothing. But might she think of applying? Of course there was no such scholarship. But it was after all his zoo. Lee applied and got it. By the end of that summer she and Gerry were engaged.

Lee was a perfect wife to Gerry. She shared his passions but was a more practical person – and very caring of Gerry. She also had quickly endeared herself to the many staff at the Wildlife Trust who were quite proprietorial about him. He, meanwhile, was every bit the larger-than-life person I had hoped for. He bursted with energy, enthusiasm and often indignation at the state of the world. And he completely adored Lee. Online I found the love letter he sent to her in 1978 in which he tells her 'I love you with a depth and passion that I have felt for no one else in this life and if this astonishes you it astonishes me as well.' It brought tears to my eyes, such was his passion. Such was also his self-awareness. This bearded, bear-like man wore his heart on his sleeve. He admitted to being overbearing and insanely jealous when it came to her. But his love was boundless. You could see that the minute you met them together. At 30, she was over 40 years his junior, but they matched beautifully and in all the years I knew them their relationship was – while often argumentative – wonderfully harmonious.

I decided it would be great if they could write a book together using his great narrative skills and Lee's brilliant research capabilities. Then, out of the blue, I was approached by an editor called Joss at Dorling Kindersley. She wanted Gerry to write a wonderfully accessible illustrated book called *The Amateur Naturalist*. He and Lee loved the idea. We did the deal and in 1982 it was published all over the world. It later became a charming television series.

In 1982 Alex and I had moved to Oxford and had our first child Alice. I remember the Durrells coming there on their promotional tour. We had arranged to have dinner the night before his Blackwell's launch. Sadly Alex was away. Lee said would I mind joining up with Gerry's old friend Desmond Morris and his wife, Ramona, who lived in North Oxford. Would I mind? Ever since reading *The Naked Ape* – the publishing sensation of the late 60s – I had been in awe of someone who could write accessible science like that. Desmond had suggested the Quat' Saisons in Summertown – run by the starry young chef Raymond Blanc, who had opened it four years before. As Gerry and Lee were great gourmets this was perfect.

I can still see the scene: these two old friends, both giants in the world of zoology and conservation who had known and respected each other for many years, sat there reminiscing and telling the most jaw-dropping stories about their experiences in the world of wildlife. It was such a privilege to witness. At one point they were talking of their great mutual friend David Attenborough and Desmond began telling us how the Attenboroughs had visited them on Gozo when Desmond was living there as a tax exile. He began describing David taking them on a flint-hunting expedition with his little hammer. It was a wonderful shaggy dog story. And I remember him saying: 'The great thing about David is that he is still at heart a hugely enthusiastic and brilliant 14-year-old. He's never lost that.' And I thought that that description applied equally to Gerry and Desmond. Gerry certainly had never lost that wide-eyed enthusiasm for everything to do with nature and also that sense of righteous indignation when nature is threatened. It never left him.

Gerry's generosity was boundless. He loved giving lavish meals and on several occasions we visited him and Lee on holiday in Le Mazet, their rambling house near Nimes in the South of France. I have a vivid picture of rotund Gerry with my tiny six-year-old Max walking over the hills with their butterfly nets. Years later when I set up my agency in Oxford, I had to leave Gerry and Lee behind. I had worked with them for ten amazing and successful years. But the Durrells had always been at Curtis Brown and all his backlist was there. We kept in touch though.

Then I remember the day in 1995 when I heard that Gerry had died. I was so very upset. He had not looked after that bulky body of his well but

I could not imagine the world without his great spirit. He was a towering figure in my life. I walked out into North Parade to go for a little walk and absorb my news. I had nobody to share it with. Then who should I bump into but Desmond Morris. So we went on a companionable walk together talking about Gerry. Afterwards I took him back to my office and showed Gerry's 'Illustrated Letter' sent to me from France years ago when he had had his first warning 'mini' heart attack. It is framed on the wall, illustrated with the enchanting cartoon animals with which anyone who got his entrancing Christmas cards would be familiar. It reads:

FELICITY!

Agent who fulfills my needs,
I've just received your kindly screeds –
Received by me with joy unbounded –
But now to prove that I am feeling better,
Send <u>you</u> an ILLUSTRATED LETTER!

What to say of La Belle France
Where arteries never have a chance?
Where every menu points with glee
The way to adiposity;
With all that wine and crispy bread…
(One more coronary – I'm dead).

Mushrooms, big as white umbrellas –
They're minus <u>calories</u> they tell us –
But simmered slow in wine and cream:

Dieter's nightmare! Glutton's dream!
But roasted truffles are the best…
(What's that hammering in my chest?).

Shall I speak of hen or duckling,
Quails and pigeons, pigs still suckling?
They <u>say</u> these things make you obese,
Like livers from whole flocks of geese
Moving like huge drifts of snow…
(One more coronary to go).

Oh how the veg's make you tremble
When in the markets they assemble:
Crisp green lettuce, dark green bean,
Shining eggplant, quite obscene,
Cooked in wine and oil and butter…
(My heart then gave a tiny flutter).

Now the fruits – they're <u>all</u> in season,
Enough to undermine one's reason.
Strawberry, peaches, merry cherry
And grapes, most subtle of the berry –
A berry you can drink <u>and</u> eat…
(Oh, damn, my heart then missed a beat).

Do not think these other dishes
Have dragged my mind away from fishes –

Salmon, rouget, turbot stout
Vie with carp and bream and trout,
While lobster red and ecrevisse...
(A heart attach's a quick release).

To moisten all this provender
Wines that leave you in a blur:
Whites like blondes at St. Tropez,
Reds that sap your will away,
Champagnes into goblets rustle...
(Hear my arteries a-bustle).

Ah! Belle France, you promised land,
Come, we'll walk now, hand in hand

With oyster, snail and bread and butter
And vintages to make you stutter;

Creamy cheese that eats so well
(Or others with atrocious smell);

Hams and salmon, sunset pink,
Fiery Armagnac to drink;

The wrinkled walnut, sugared marron,
Where'er we walk you are not barren:

You fill my glass, you pile my plate,
'Tis you who've got me in this state.

Belle France, I love you, there's no doubt,
But one thing I must just point out –

That here and now I do attest
YOU caused my cardiac arrest!

ENVOI

Felicity, my dearest girl,
Do not cast me as a churl,
But I must end, cast down my quill,
Assuring you I love you still –
So please don't think of me a sinner –
But – seven o'clock –

It's time for dinner.

All my love
Gerry

[At this point, Felicity had noted the names of other authors whom she represented, intending to write about them, but had not done so before she died.]

15.

1979–81

In late May of 1979 I was attending BookExpo in Los Angeles and grabbed the opportunity of a weekend in Washington on the way back. I stayed with Larry. We were not lovers, just loving best friends. He had had what sounded like a very happy relationship with one Susan – to whom his one and only book *The Wrong Horse* is dedicated. But that had come to a sad end. I had a friend in England, a businessman called Cob, with whom I shared a passion for opera and gardens and whose life was quite fascinating. But I could not pretend that I was in love. I was also I think still feeling wounded by my parting from Alasdair. So my visit was a tonic, being with Larry and catching up with friends.

Ben Bradlee and Sally Quinn were now married and living next door to Larry and were plotting his fiftieth birthday party in two weeks' time on 17 June. Surely I could come back for that? It was tempting. Then I visited Peter and Margaret Jay at the British Embassy. Margaret's father Jim Callaghan had appointed Peter as British ambassador to Washington in 1977 so they had been there two years. But Mrs Thatcher had become Prime Minister in May, so they would be leaving the embassy in late summer. They were giving their Farewell Ball on 23 June. Why did I not come over for Larry's party and then stay with them for a week in the Residence and come to the ball? It was all too good an offer. So that's what I did.

The day before Larry's party saw me back in Washington and helping Ben and Sally prepare. Ben and I drove out to a plant nursery in Bethesda and bought Larry a special red maple tree for his front yard. I have two great pictures: one of Larry with Ben and one of Larry with me by that tree. I don't remember much of the party except that it was full of people I was fond of. Then I spent much of the week lingering with Larry and friends and having a very merry time with Peter and Margaret in the grandeur of the Embassy Residence. My album shows photos of Larry's children, Marc and Cathy – she now married with a baby – and of Wyche Fowler, who was now a dapper-looking congressman for Atlanta, with his old girlfriend, Eleanor Randolph – who I had first met in London in 1972 when she worked for the *St. Petersburg Times* in Florida and was by now working on the *Washington Post*. The Jays' ball was magnificent. I wore my Marisa Martin dress and danced the night away with Larry. Then on Sunday night I flew home.

In mid-August Cob and I were staying the weekend with his great friends Bob and Nicky Gavron in Sussex. We came back late on Sunday to many messages for me on his answerphone. Joe Rogaly was the one I called first. They had been trying to find me. Larry had had a heart attack on Saturday running with friends in Martha's Vineyard. He was dead. His memorial meeting would be in Washington on Tuesday. Looking back, I marvel at my calm. I booked a cheap Laker Airlines flight to New York the next day connecting to DC, arranged to stay Monday and Tuesday night with John and Elizabeth Midgley and with the dawn I remember tossing off a 500-word gardening piece for the *Standard*, which I could post from the airport.

At Heathrow I was still thinking that this was not happening. And it got worse. My flight was cancelled. All I can remember was that I got a later flight, missed the last connection in New York for Washington and ended up in tears among the tramps at Penn Station. From there I took a Greyhound bus through the night to Washington.

The memorial was packed. People had come from all over America, all stunned by the loss. Larry had no religion and it took place in a large but simple Quaker meeting room close to Dupont Circle. Ben Bradlee was in charge and the speakers included Izzy Stone. It was a rather male line-up. But Sally and I joined and both spoke. I remember little of what I said except that – as the Rev. Wrigley had said of my mother – that I knew I was a better person for having known Larry. The final speaker was a young man who had worked with Larry on the National Desk. He was Jewish. Larry had been his teacher – his rabbi. And then he broke into a wailing account of the Kaddish – the Jewish funeral prayer – which allowed those of us who were not already crying to do so.

Then a group of us lunched down the road at Larry's favourite joint, Nora's, and the southerner Phil Carter bellowed his rage. And Willie Shawcross turned up from England. That evening there were drinks on Katherine Graham's terrace on the roof of the *Washington Post* building downtown. In the *Post* Ben had written, 'His paper and his friends will be a long time getting over the loss of Larry Stern. He was a world class journalist. He wrote like a dream, with grace and precision. His commitment to excellence, to his staff, to his friends and to the *Washington Post* will be an example for all of us.' As the party ended Ben made an impassioned toast to his dearest friend and threw his glass against the wall. We all followed suit – and the bill for 150-odd glasses was framed outside Ben's office door for eternity.

Larry's death was a watershed for me. His love and concern for my happiness had been a constant. It showed starkly that my present relationship was not satisfactory. My diary for 1980 is missing. But come the spring that was over and in the summer I had an affair with a journalist from Hong Kong. And while I certainly had an interesting time zipping backwards and forwards on Cathay Pacific and writing pieces for the *Economist* on the Hong Kong printing trade, we were not meant for the longer term.

The one wonderful thing that emerged from Larry's death and which has kept him in my life ever since was the Stern Fellowship. In the November after Larry died Godfrey Hodgson gave me a call. He had been one of Larry's closest British friends and still spent much time in Washington researching and writing books. He had just come from Washington where he had seen Ben Bradlee. They had had an idea – of which he hoped I approved – that they would set up a fellowship in Larry's memory. Every year a young British journalist would be selected to spend three summer months working on the National Desk of the *Washington Post* and then a month travelling wherever they wished. I remember crying, so moved was I. For it seemed so totally appropriate. Larry had always encouraged young journalists and he had always admired British journalism. Godfrey was pleased I liked the idea as he proposed that he and I would be joint 'secretaries', selecting a group of Larry's old friends who would be our selection committee and start fundraising.

So that's what we did. And in 1980 David Leigh from the *Guardian* was our first Stern Fellow. A starry cast have followed, including Jim Naughtie, Lionel Barber, Gary Younge, Ian Katz, Cathy Newman and Louisa Loveluck – 40 in all. Our first selection committee included Godfrey, Bruce Page – his old sparring partner on the *Sunday Times* Insight Team – my old flame David Watt, William Shawcross, Anthony Sampson, John Freeman, Harry Evans and Bob Jones, and we were later joined by Victoria Brittain. Bob was Godfrey's idea as he was an ex-*Sunday Times* reporter who was just setting up the School of Journalism at City University. The Stern Fellowship would have a base there and we could hold our meetings there. It has been a great association. I remember the first year that Ben came over to select from our shortlist. He was given an honorary doctorate at the university and gave the most robust and inspiring lecture.

As years have gone on we have added alumni to the selection process to keep us in touch with contemporary journalism – and the tradition of the editor coming over to make his selection and giving a great party for the alumni while he is at it is continued today by Marty Baron.

[*Two weeks before she died, Felicity was delighted to learn that the Stern Fellowship was renamed the Stern-Bryan Fellowship.*]

By now I had moved house. Returning to Mayton Street had very much felt like going backwards. I was lucky to have the bolt-hole. But since I was clearly not going to move in with Cob in his glorious Highgate home in The Grove, I started looking around. I found the most perfect two-storey maisonette comprising the ground and first floors of a white stucco house at 7 Priory Road – what the estate agents called 'Leafy St John's Wood Borders'. It had a large square garden with a breathtaking pear tree. And while the garden was covered in concrete stones, its potential was terrific. I remember sitting in the elegantly proportioned first-floor sitting room with its floor-to-ceiling Georgian windows – next to the equally elegantly proportioned garden-facing bedroom – looking across the quiet street to the house opposite – coincidentally occupied by my old friend Derry Irvine – and thinking, 'I wouldn't mind growing old here.'

So I bought it in late 1979, got an excellent design from my author John Brookes, and started doing up the garden right away. It features in my book *The Town Gardener's Companion*, which is really a collection of my *Evening Standard* articles arranged by month and which I wrote in Priory Road after I stopped my *Evening Standard* column.

Meanwhile my step-brother Alex had returned from his four years in Sudan, complete with World Bank savings, and had acquired a house in Oakthorpe Road in Summertown, north Oxford. He loved Oxford and, particularly with his aunt Deb living there, it was the place where he felt he had the most roots. He had a girlfriend, Louise, who was heavily involved in helping him with the decor, and was generally feeling very upbeat. He planned to base himself there working as an independent agricultural economist.

I remember that summer having tea with Deb and she suddenly announced that she hoped Alex would not marry Louise. Deb is always a person of strong opinions and I don't recall how Louise had blotted her copy-book. What I do recall is my reaction: 'But Alex is far too young to get married!' 'He's 30,' said Deb. 'Young men at 30 start thinking about getting married.'

That summer my grandmother Mardy had a fall. Every week she attended communion in the local Fulford church on a Wednesday. Why Wednesday? 'Well, my dear, it's because they use the old prayer book. It's not that I mind the new one, it's just that I know the old one by heart and don't have to use my specs. There we are – the blind, the halt, the lame – the Wednesday crowd.' When I asked her once if she sat next to her great friend Mrs Durnford in church she said, in some shock, 'Oh no! We both sit alone. We like to feel that we are surrounded by our families.' She had outlived her husband and both her children and that was when she peacefully communed with them. I've often thought of that – for I sometimes feel the same.

One Wednesday morning she was making her way up the aisle to receive her communion. To her surprise, the substantial Mr Pike gave her his arm – and she didn't like to say no. Up front there she stood, arms outstretched to receive the host, when suddenly Mr Pike 'had one of his turns'. He fell heavily, sending Mardy reeling across the choir. Being the Wednesday crowd there were none strong enough to help and the young vicar had to abandon bread and wine to peel Mr Pike off. Gran still insisted on having her communion before going back to her seat. But come the end of the service she could not get up. She had cracked her pelvis and was rushed off to hospital. Mr Pike came to, unaware of the damage he had done.

This happened when my friend Robert from Hong Kong was staying for a romantic weekend. So plans had to change. Libby called. She was rushing up from London. Could I go on Sunday? So the surprised Robert's weekend included a visit to York. I went to see Gran alone first. There she sat in elegance, a haze of lace boleros, in a big ward surrounded by ton-up boys (motorcycle junkies of the time) who had crashed their bikes. By the time I arrived she knew the life histories of her neighbours and was feeling sociable. So, having walked the walls of York with Robert and shown him the Minster (always a total pleasure), I took him back to meet Gran for tea.

She greeted him warmly. 'Robert lives in Hong Kong,' I said. 'How interesting,' she replied. 'I have always longed to go to the Far East. Tell me about your life in Hong Kong.' She later said, 'And do you know Thailand?' Indeed he did; in fact, he had been there most recently with me. 'I have a great friend from Thailand called Nepa,' she said – Nepa had been my sister's lodger. 'She is such a wonderful girl. But she lacks self-confidence and I feel it has something to do with her Buddhism. You see, I got this book from the library called *Buddhism Explained* and it's not at all like *our* religion. There is nothing to hold on to.' Whereupon she delivered a talk on Buddha and his life – disapproving strongly of him abandoning his family – and the difficulty and vagueness of achieving Nirvana. And I sat there feeling so proud of Mardy, who at 95 had taken the trouble to study Buddhism in order to better understand her new friend.

Late in the year I saw Alex in Oxford. He was planning to go to the Gambia in December for four months with a group of colleagues to prepare a food security strategy. He was looking forward to it. He asked what I was doing for Christmas. My Far Eastern romance was over. I had no plans and was feeling quite sorry for myself. Why not come to the Gambia? They would have a large house with lots of space. I said it was sweet of him but I could not afford it – all that jetting to Hong Kong had not come cheap. He would pay, he said with that wonderful expansive gesture I have come to know so well. As it turned out, the *Evening Standard*, for whom I still periodically wrote travel pieces, welcomed the idea of an article on a place that, with its magic beaches, was becoming more popular with tourists, and was comparatively close for a winter break. So that solved my flight.

On 22 December I flew to Banjul for two weeks. Luckily my 1981 diary is to hand. And this eventful date begins it. Alex's colleagues – Peter Stutley, Richard Longhurst and Jennie Dey – were excellent company. The house was charming and capacious and included a friendly and endearing dog called Fido. They were working by day and I see I made my token visit to the Tourism Ministry. This was my first trip to West Africa and I remember being particularly struck by the joyous atmosphere, which was very different from what I had felt in former colonial countries I had visited in East Africa. Was it because the British had never settled in West Africa that there was no feeling of the master/ servant tradition, which I always felt in, for instance, Kenya? Whatever the reason, I found the Gambians particularly outgoing and warm to me and I revelled in their streets and markets.

On Christmas Eve we went to the midnight service in Banjul Cathedral. On Christmas morning dancers were celebrating in the street and we took ourselves off to a beachside picnic. Jennie Dey had done the fieldwork for her thesis in the Gambia and some days later, as part of a four-day work trip up the Gambia River, we visited Saruja, the village where she had lived. I could not imagine choosing to live somewhere so very basic. The river journey was glorious and you understood why so many European birdwatchers made the Gambia their destination.

All this time I had been observing Alex at work. I had been so impressed by him, by the way he related to the Gambians he was working with and by the considered way he explained the problems of the farmers to me. Of course I had seen Alex at work before but this time I began to feel a great attraction. This was no longer my warm, endearing kid-brother. This was a very impressive man. Anyway, whatever the reason, my vision of Alex shifted. When we had first met he had been an Oxford undergraduate of 20 and I a 24-year-old sophisticated reporter living in London. I had felt a great deal older than him. Now our age difference did not matter a jot. Anyway, it was on New Year's Eve that I realised with a tingle that I was in love with my step-brother ... My holiday certainly shifted a gear.

Then back I flew on 6 January. I see that I lunched with my father on Friday, 9 January, and presumably I will have told him that Alex and I were now an item. I know he was really pleased because he rated Alex very highly. But he must have been a touch apprehensive about what Cynthia would think. But Cynthia soon had other matters to think about. Annie in Washington announced that she was getting married to Akbar Noman, an economist and former work colleague who came from Pakistan and who I had met with her the previous June when I had my Washington week. Alex called me from Banjul. He was planning to go to Washington for the wedding on 30 January and of course I was going to go too.

Sometime in mid-January Annie flew to London with Akbar and took him on a whistle-stop tour of all the relatives – including visiting me in Priory Road. I immediately found him wonderfully warm and funny and could absolutely see the attraction. I have always adored Akbar. But I did wonder what Cynthia was making of him. He was divorced. So any dreams she had of presiding over her daughter's white wedding were out the window. Akbar and I have always felt a particular bond as the son- and daughter-in-law who Cynthia would NOT have picked.

So Alex and I met up in Washington on 30 January at the house of my old friend Eleanor Randolph, by now married to the British journalist Peter Pringle, where we were staying. Eleanor was delighted to be involved in this clandestine romance. Alex had had a considerable adventure making it from Banjul to Washington, missing a ferry on the way, but had got to the wedding on the Friday – performed by a rent-a-priest who they had found in the *Yellow Pages*. Cynthia was there and had apparently spent the journey to the ceremony asking Annie if she was absolutely sure ... I arrived for the evening party, a wonderful gathering of their international friends. Alex had to leave the next day and I have photos of Annie, Akbar and me walking in Rock Creek Park on a sunny afternoon and feeling very happy with life.

The other day I said to Alex: 'When did we decide to get married?' To which he replied that it had 'sort of crept up on us'. We had had the tricky conversation about how Cynthia would take the news and Alex was very firm. He knew his mother could be difficult and had a long time ago resolved that if it was a choice between the woman he wanted to marry and his mother's opinion, there would be no doubt. Cynthia would just have to come round.

Alex returned from the Gambia at the end of March. There was a weekend at Park Farm, probably Easter, when Alex and I went up. We were going to some dinner party and Alex drove Cynthia and Papa drove me. That's when Alex told Cynthia that we were together and wanted to get married. And her comment was: 'I always hoped you would have married Alice Lobb.'

To give Cynthia her due, by the time we announced our engagement in July her response was that it was splendid and what could she do to help with the wedding. And from then on she changed. I can't pretend we became immediately close – there was too much water under that bridge. But we both made an effort and years later as Alice, Max and Ben arrived she proved herself the most attentive, dutiful and loving granny. It also affected the way she treated my sisters – as if, strangely, we had all become honorary Duncans.

Certainly by the time of the Royal Wedding at the end of July it was public knowledge as I remember Alex's grandmother Kathleen bringing out the champagne at Hexton, which I had assumed was for us but was for the Royal Couple ...

This is when the photo albums begin. We had a glorious summer trickling through France staying with Patrick and his wife-to-be Alison Phillips in the Camargue and then accompanying them on a magic walk with the local shepherd taking his sheep and goats on the transhumance up into the Alps. It was a period of enchantment I shall remember all my life, fruitlessly chasing sheep to keep them from eating orchids and the primrose-coloured foxgloves. It was also the first of so many adventures or just happy times we have had hanging out with Patrick and his enchanting Alison, who I simply love.

And so we married on 23 October 1981 and that very morning discovered that I was pregnant. We moved into the Old Rectory in Kidlington on 11 June 1983 – Alice's first birthday – and with me pregnant with Max. Ben followed in 1987. We have had a good life here. We have relished each other's company and it has been a happy home. We have had huge tragedies. Our charming Alice killed herself in 2004, suffering from the manic depression that had blighted my mother; Bunny, only ordained as a priest the year before and with two small children, Liz and Catherine, died in 1995 of ovarian cancer, showing that the wretched BRCA1 gene in my father's family had hit our generation; Libby died of pancreatic cancer in 2008 (also BRCA1-related); I am now suffering from my fourth cancer and have Alex, Max and Ben looking after me. But despite all this I do feel that I have had a very good life.

Alex has always been my stalwart. When, after Ben was born, it was clear that my life commuting could not go on it was he who encouraged me to start my own literary agency in Oxford with him as my business partner. Twenty years on he helped me with my management buyout so I was able to hand over the reins to Catherine Clarke and all my fantastic colleagues. Somebody once said to Caroline Wood that Felicity Bryan Associates is known as the happiest agency. And they were right. Certainly I find it hard to think of leaving. But Alex is here and it is wonderful to have a partner who always sees you at your best.

Index

A

Abed, Fazle Hasan, 108, 138, 139, 140
Amalfi coast, Italy, 160
America, 49, 50, 52, 53, 54, 55, 56, 59,
 60, 61, 63, 71, 75, 86, 88, 89, 147,
 154, 179, 188, 197
Amin, President Idi, 132, 133
Angkor Wat, 93, 97
Anguilla, 77, 78, 79
Arts Briefs (of the *Economist*), 7, 109
Ashley Cooper, Anne, 119
Ashley Cooper, Jim, 119
Ashley Cooper, Kathleen, 206
Assisi, 31
Atlanta Georgia, 73, 81, 196
Atlas, James, 187
Attenborough, David, 190
Austria, 34

B

Bailey, Jim, 133
Baker, Jeremy, 54
Balfour, Nancy, 91, 105, 106
Ballet, 5, 22, 24, 25, 32, 42, 53, 99, 109
Bangkok, 101, 123
Bangladesh, 108, 138, 139, 140
Banteay Srei, 98
Barber, Lionel, 199
Barber, Tony, 17
Baring, Diana (nee Crawfurd), 114, 149,
 150, 151
Baron, Marty, 199
Barraclough, Jenny and Michael, 157
Barraclough, Rachael, 12
Beale, Margaret (Muggs), 24, 26, 27,
 39, 159
Beauman, Christopher, 134, 135, 136,
 137, 138